Theopoetics

Theopoetics

*Spiritual Poetry for Contemplative
Theology and Daily Living*

Phillip Michael Garner

FOREWORD BY
Shaun Galford

WIPF & STOCK · Eugene, Oregon

THEOPOETICS
Spiritual Poetry for Contemplative Theology and Daily Living

Wipf & Stock
An Imprint of Wipf and Stock Publishers
199 W. 8th Ave., Suite 3
Eugene, OR 97401

www.wipfandstock.com

PAPERBACK ISBN: 978-1-5326-1829-1
HARDCOVER ISBN: 978-1-4982-4374-2
EBOOK ISBN: 978-1-4982-4373-5

Manufactured in the U.S.A.

Table of Contents

The Tower of Futility

The People of God

Faith a Tangible Reality

Interviewing Wisdom

More than a Feeling

A Little Wickedness

Love is Holiness

In Honor of an Exemplary People

Little Human Beings

Foreword

Shaun Galford

Mike Garner's newest book, *Theopoetics: Spiritual Poetry for Contemplative Theology and Daily Living*, is truly an inspired work. Those familiar with Mike's first two books may be surprised his newest is free verse poetry that specifically addresses theological thought. Although *Everyday Thoughts* contains a number of Mike's poems, there is a definitive difference in the subject matter and style of poetry in *Theopoetics*. This not only reflects the aspect of Mike's personality that gravitates toward newness and possibility, but also a strong faith to take a chance, believing that the Lord would use him to serve others through this medium. We live in a society where people play it safe, not wanting to risk doing something unpredictable for fear that the endeavor could be a waste of time. Sadly, too often our tendency to "play it safe" inhibits us from realizing our full potential. However, Mike's confidence to venture into unfamiliar territory and enhance his capacity as a teacher by learning the art of poetry for the benefit of others is a model for the rest of us.

Mike is a theological educator through and through, which is why he could not write poetry for the sake of simply writing poetry, but rather he found in it a way to pack in layers of theology and meaning; hence the nuance—Theopoetics. Readers familiar with Scripture will hear echoes of the Biblical prophets on the pages that follow. Each piece is carefully crafted; not a word is wasted. Throughout this collection of poetic writing, Scriptural allusions abound. The poetry in this book is infused with truth telling. As you peel away the layers of meaning you will be challenged to face reality, even the suffering that is part of the human experience. Mike chose a while ago to embrace human frailty and walk in obedience to Christ.

When asked to write this foreword, I was both honored and humbled by the request. I've had the opportunity to be a student of Mr. Garner for a over a decade in both non-formal and formal settings, from community Bible studies to graduate courses at the Institute for Global Outreach Developments Int'l, where he was founding director and dean. In addition, our relationship extended beyond the classroom to doing ministry together, both in the U.S. and the Philippines. He and I have walked through the slums of the Philippines, preached in jails, ministered to girls victimized by the horrors of the sex slave industry, fed children living on the street, wrestled with the problem of worker exploitation in developing nations by global corporations, and hiked into the mountains to visit the Aeta an indigenous population of tribal people who are marginalized in the larger society. We've had many conversations about life and ministry in these contexts. I've long appreciated his willingness to tell me the truth and share the wisdom he's gleaned through study of the Bible and his experience as a missionary.

I actually first met Mike outside the U.S. when I was 25 years old on a mission trip to Ensenada, Mexico. He was working alongside his son to help lead a sizeable team to serve the poor in that area. In those days I was unaware of the impact he'd have on my life as a teacher and friend. My earliest memory of him was outside the local church where we stayed. As we waited for lunch to be served, Gregg, Mike's son, was sharing about how much his father enjoyed discussing the Bible. Shortly thereafter we were eating our meal, one of my friends who had been part of that previous conversation turned to Mike and asked a question unrelated to the Bible. Mike gave no response, but just stared intently at the young man who quietly went back to eating his meal. The young man assumed that the lack of response was due to the fact his question had nothing at all to do with the Bible. He thought to himself, "If I'm going to talk to Mr. Garner, I better have a question that relates to the Bible, otherwise I'll just keep quiet." Later, the young man learned Mike didn't respond because he didn't hear him due to impaired hearing, a problem he lived with for a number of years before getting hearing aids as a gift for his 50th birthday. The hearing issues are likely due to working on helicopters during his years in the Marine Corp and the constant cling and clatter of tools and machinery from years of doing construction and plumbing. It wasn't that Mike didn't care about the young man's question; he just didn't hear him. While there is a comedic element to that story, his son was right, Mike puts priority on learning, discussing, and applying Scripture to life (ethical conversation).

Although Mike is a professor of Masters level theology courses at the Institute of GOD Int'l, it's a common scene to find him sitting down outside the class with a group of students in the lounge area of our campus talking Bible and telling stories. Yet, it doesn't stop there. Mike is known for engaging in theological discussion in a variety of venues, from having weekly conversations with his son over coffee, in the sauna at the local YMCA or through social media. People interested in the Bible tend to gravitate to him. This is not to say Mike doesn't enjoy times for light, playful bantering. He has what he calls "hevel time," playing off the Hebrew word, which means vanity. However, those times are far from vanity, but instead an opportunity for relationship building. And what often begins with joking turns into a time of storytelling.

In his poem "Tell Me a Story: When Storytellers Rule the World," he highlights the power of a story to impact the world. And that all of us, because we are children of God, can approach each day as a new opportunity to participate in the story God is writing through the lives of the faithful. We all can be saints, but it comes on the other side of making the choice to obey. When I read that poem, I get the sense that telling the story of a life lived for God that brings peace in the world is far more potent than any glory related to military conquest. Unfortunately, the latter are the stories that litter most history books. Young people are kept from hearing about truly heroic individuals. Theologians should be storytellers, because a story can change the world.

The exemplary soul models their kerygma; it is embodied in their life of service to the poor and oppressed through the stories they speak. The narrative piece that expounds that poem is written about how in large part the current state of academia has been reduced to vanity (hevel), being more concerned with intellectual technique and the privileged access they have to learning and information.

It didn't take me long to recognize that theology is the lens whereby Mike interprets the world. It's quite evident that his perspective is shaped by faith in God and his reading of Scripture. The Bible should inform our perspective, from the practical ways in which we love those around us and in response to the systemic issues with an impact that has reached global proportions, causing pain and suffering to those most vulnerable. We live in an age where there is a growing disparity between rich and poor due to the rampant greed that marks this imperial age, when so many who remain voiceless are dying unnecessarily. In his poem, *Prophetic Denunciation: When Prophets Weep*, which is undoubtedly influenced by Mike's years of study and teaching books like Hosea, Amos, and Jeremiah, he writes,

> *"Laid at the gate of a globalized world*
> *are the children of Lazarus*
> *Capitalism displays contempt for life*
> *Empire is indicative of God's absence*
> *there is no hiding."*

During a historical moment when so many people are deprived the good things God intends for them, the world needs more theologians that will speak and write words of "prophetic denunciation," awakening us to our need for the presence of God, which will come when we return and begin to care for those laying at our gates.

Anyone reading Mike's books will get the sense that he believes it's vanity to divorce theological concepts from the lives we are expected to live in Christ. To quote one of the writers and thinkers that has influenced him, Rabbi Abraham Joshua Heschel says in his important work, *The Prophets*, "God himself is described as reflecting over the plight of man rather than as contemplating eternal ideas." Indeed, one of the first things Mike taught me in the classroom was that "Christianity is meant to be lived, not simply learned about." I've carried this pedagogical statement with me over the years, as it has helped ground me in ethical responsibility to my friends, family, and neighbor. The statement itself, as well as the heart behind it, I've passed on to students in my history and theology classes. When I teach courses on the History of Christianity, this statement is a key component of the criteria we use to find those characters, the cloud of witnesses, that were faithful and walked worthy of the vocation to which they were called.

Mike lives out what he teaches, reflected in a lifetime spent in ministerial service as pastor, missionary and teacher. Serving the Lord is not something you retire from, but rather a lifetime commitment. In the poem "A Life Built on a Rock: Conviction," he writes,

"I'm older now

My sail flies a little higher

The wind remains unpredictable

Perhaps it's time to walk on water

One more time"

The above lines reflect the deep conviction he has of making himself available to the Lord as he ages. Aging makes us face our vulnerability and weakness as human beings. We literally start to decay and death becomes an enemy. In regards to death, I've often heard Mike say, "Nobody gets out alive." Mike is now 61 years old and he has seen and experienced suffering.

As a young person in the Marine Corp arriving in Olongapo City in the 1970s in the waning years of the Vietnam War, Mike witnessed the incredible injustices and abuses of the American Empire's complicity in the "sex industry," which has become increasingly globalized. It was there that Mike would meet his first wife, Trinidad, a young woman who was a victim of the U.S. military presence. The disparity of wealth between U.S. forces and the poverty of the local population brought on the tendency for the powerful to injure the powerless to satisfy their errant desires. When I took Jeremiah class with Mr. Garner he taught that the human "propensity for evil" surprised God. Olongapo City was known as 'sin city' and the home to unhindered sexual activity unlike anywhere else in the world.

Not only has Mike witnessed the suffering of others, but he too has experienced physical limitations and pain, from the premature hearing loss to complete hip replacement surgery in his fifties. For years, Mike endured the pain associated with two bad hips. He would sit teaching in a classroom multiple hours everyday, rubbing his leg and enduring pain but focused on students growing in their knowledge of the Lord.

When Mike says, "My sail flies a little higher," I'm provoked to think about the pursuit that most people have in our society to retire someplace warm and sunny. They buy a boat and sail out to sea, attempting to live a dream of eternal youth. However, the imagery in this poem is Biblical, causing us to think about the "Stilling of the Storm" story in the synoptic Gospels. As Jesus and the disciples sail to the other side of the lake the chaotic, unpredictable storm hits. Life is always unpredictable and times of chaos are inevitable. Aging makes us feel even more vulnerable to the unpredictability of life, and the human tendency is self-preservation. Thus, we pursue control and power in our futile efforts to keep death away. Jesus gave us another option, and that's to get in the boat with him, which is riskier and requires faith. Mike says, "Human beings were not meant to walk on water. Yet, at the invitation of Jesus a few steps are a life changing experience."

Someone in a boat over the open water feels more vulnerable than the one on land. However, Jesus shows no fear or doubt in the story. He can sleep through the storm, calm it with his words, believing the whole time that no matter what happens, if it's the will of the father, he'll reach the other side. Yet, the journey doesn't stop there, because chaos, manifested in a human being, an archetype, dehumanized from the effects of war meets us on the other side. So it was in the gospel, when Jesus and the disciples disembark from the boat and encounter a demonized man whose identity reflects the horror and presence of the Roman legions upon the populace. The faith Jesus' displays, he expects from us, his followers. So, when I read this line in Mike's poetry, I hear a man facing the limits of human mortality, but choosing the option of faith over fear, and putting himself out there once more to get in that boat with Jesus, maybe take a few steps onto the water. We just don't retire from our service to the Lord. Despite Mike's physical challenges, he continues to live out his calling. Shortly after this book is published, Mike will be setting sail for the Philippines once again. This time to live out the rest of his life in Asia, write books, and bring his knowledge to the those thirsty for moral readings of scripture.

Mike Garner is above all a theological educator concerned that his students draw closer to the Lord. I remember seeing him in the Institute for G.O.D. Int'l library one day after classes. We were having a brief conversation about all the books and the acquisition of knowledge. I made a comment reflecting my desire to learn all that I could from the books on the shelves, but he responded to me that developing a relationship with the Lord should be prioritized over all the knowledge contained in those books. At the same time, Mike is inspired and motivated by ideas and concepts. If he reads a book and finds one idea or principle that is beneficial and enriching, then the time spent reading he considers valuable. When Mike learns something that is good, he then wants to give it away to others. Historically, there has been an issue with theologians hoarding knowledge. However, a teacher in service to Jesus Christ will share their knowledge of God. In the passage typically referred to as the 'Great Commission,' Jesus commands his disciples to 'teach' the nations all that he commanded them.

One of the first Bible classes I took at the Institute was Biblical Interpretation. It was a class that Mike taught, and it covered the books of Hosea and Amos. I was very disturbed to learn one of the major issues was how the theologians of the day, the priests, were depriving the people from the knowledge of God. This problem repeats throughout history. During the middle ages this was called "obscurantism," the withholding of knowledge to keep people in the dark. In that class, I came to realize how the knowledge of God filling my soul and mind was replacing unhealthy ideas.

Theopoetics is Mike Garner's third published work following *Interpretive Adventures: Subversive Readings in a Missional School* and Everyday Thoughts: *A Collection of Devotional Readings for Thinking Christians.* In *Interpretive Adventures* he puts forward fresh and insightful readings of Scripture in order to help believers live out their faith and particularly those who have a missional calling. Mike's contributions to Biblical hermeneutics carry the authority that comes from years of experience as a teacher and missionary. Although he would not claim to be a wordsmith, anyone that reads *Interpretive Adventures* would be impacted by Mike's pithy theological statements; each convey a depth of theological meaning. For instance, in dealing with the plague narratives in Exodus, he writes, "When God Liberates, Look for Mercy." He puts forward a prophetic reading that highlights the mercy of God in a passage that many use to argue God is controlling and vengeful. I appreciate the ability to pack such a liberating teaching about God into a concise statement that can be unpacked and discussed.

Mike's subtitle in Everyday Thoughts, *A Collection of Devotional Readings for thinking Christians,* reflects his frustration and response to the mass proliferation of Christian devotionals that don't engage our mind and thus leave us Spiritually dwarfed. The shift to devotional writing reflects Mike's versatility as a theological educator and writer.

Reflected clearly in the title of the second book, but definitely a major part of his first and recent work, is his concern for Christians to engage God with their mind. The absence of critical thinking in popular Christianity is a major issue. When people cannot think for themselves then they will follow the crowd. Mike taught in Gospels class "crowds are fickle." One minute they love Jesus and they next they are yelling "crucify him!" In order to act according to God's word, it's necessary that it become the source of constant meditations. For years, Mike has challenged me and his other students to think more deeply. The expectation "in Christ" is that our thoughts would mature. The unfortunate reality, however, is that most folks, including, and perhaps especially Christians, don't know how to think. We don't just need devotionals to connect us emotionally to God, but also to engage our minds in worship. Mike tried to address this issue with "Everyday Thoughts".

Not thinking makes us more susceptible to the common ideologies of the day, which leads us to a life of materialistic consumerism, militarism and nationalism. This has detrimental effects not only on us, but our children as well. When Mike entered the Marine Corp as a young man, he had not been taught that military service was incompatible with the Christian faith. Later in life, Mike experienced the revelation that Jesus was nonviolent, and in that case his followers should be too. An ethic of nonviolence should be a core value for the people of God. A way we move towards society where "swords are beat into plowshares" is by teaching our children not to participate in violent activity, including any form of military service. In the poem, "Christian Resistance: World Creators," he writes,

"God Bless

Our children to resist

not with weapons or fists

but with wisdom and one another

Freedom of speech is impotent without
freedom of thought."

This stanza challenges the idea that blessing is evidenced by wealth and material abundance, which is the notion at the heart of the modern prosperity gospel. Again, Mike is challenging us to think, or perhaps re-think how we understand blessing. He connects it to our children. However, our progeny, the very thing that reflects God's blessing in our lives have been indoctrinated by the ideologies of our age. In the gospels Jesus says, 'wisdom is vindicated by its children,' but we live in an age where kids are taught to war, and the apex of service is to enlist in the military.

This reality is not unique to our age. The state has long fostered a spirit of nationalism to compel parents to give their children over for battle. The prophet Micah projected the vision of a new world where "children learn war no more." The first act of resistance is for parents to teach their children from a young age that military participation is not consistent with our faith. Jesus will define blessing in Matthew 5 as peacemakers who in effect are children of God. Christian resistance will happen when the next generation is taught how to speak and think with faith in a world seeking to instill in them the values of the dominant culture. Mike shares this concern and believes that by teaching our kids war is not an option and instilling in them the need to be thinking and informed persons, the world can change. They can leave off building towers and fueling the city so they can participate in the wonderful work of building Christ's kingdom that comes from knowing God and his word.

The final poem of this collection is under the heading 'Living Truth' is titled 'Freedom and Truth'. Truth is an abstract theme that has been pursued by philosophers throughout the ages. When Pilate asks Jesus, "What is truth?" He is asking a question one could hear from Plato. The irony is that Jesus was the embodiment of truth, standing before his very eyes, yet he could not see. We believe that truth is not some abstract concept, but revealed in a historical person, Jesus of Nazareth. In the poem, Mike writes,

"Truth is a disruptive power in the world

Liberation from perceived normalcy

Freedom from

Freedom to

A dizzying experience"

This makes me think about how we are all faced with whether or not we'll accept the truth of Jesus, even when it disrupts our comfort and the semblance of control we think is real. Yet, we don't even know we are slaves, slaves to ideas that keep us chained to the wall, rather than living a life 'in Christ', a life of freedom. The version of freedom we have that says do whatever you want is false. The truth is we need Jesus. He is the one that can free us from a mundane, purposeless life, so we can be free to truly live. I think it was intentional on Mike's part to leave us with this final poem, the fortieth in the collection, which challenges us to choose the living truth, rather than the false truth of freedom promoted by our culture.

A Response to the Blind

With the Eyes of God

If he touches me and opens my eyes
I shudder at the thought
To see the world with the vision of God
Like the blind man of old my vision was blurred but clearing
Is it heaven I see emerging in me

Forgive me O Lord
Seeing my blindness grips me with pain
In the eyes of my friends I have become a madman
I am as one misunderstood, an alien, an exile
Your hope has become my imagination

As you draw closer
I refuse to look away
It is your ways that I have not seen
My death comes near as my sight clears
I see a world to come living in me

With my last breath I will speak of your love
I will demand justice
Cry out for peace
Stand alongside the poor and oppressed
I was blind but now I see

"The Spirit of the Lord is upon me, because he has anointed me to bring good news to the poor. He has sent me to proclaim release to the captives and recovery of sight to the blind, to let the oppressed go free,"

Luke 4:18

Blindness

A visionless soul cannot imagine beyond the status quo. It is to this condition that Jesus applied the word blindness. The healing of this blindness results in the witness of an uncompromising life; in a person who lives the vision of an alternate reality; this is Jesus› reality, it is born of God. For this reason Christianity is more than dogma, more than reason, more than words, it is a way of living.

It is not a better argument that changes the world; it is a better life, a life marked by a power that can only be termed Spirit. A better argument is not effective because words are like spirit; they are invisible to the blind. This truth would prompt Jesus to make statements like, "Come and see" and "Follow me".

When the gospel is understood in all the fullness of its message and meaning it makes sense of reality. For this reason, communal movements toward the utopian, the ideal, the reign of God can embody a better argument for how humanity is to live, and how the world will be governed. However those arguments press against the power of normalized structures established by culture and the state.

People are in need of order, yet they should fear ordering the world offered by mandates of institutional or legal power because regulations

The loss of order is a fear that holds each individual back from embracing their power as creators of reality.

stagnate, they limit damage but do not exemplify Spirit. Of course Jesus, through his life, taught his followers to tolerate the powers of government and taxation so that they could embody a greater power; the reign of God in humanity.

Those people who acquire the most also fear the most. It is not God who they fear, but suffering. They ignore the poor and suffering because without faith, suffering is meaningless and personal or national security becomes their god. To ignore the suffering of the poor is to live unethically and defy the voice of morality that comes from God. The attempt to provide meaning through acquisition, through self-empowerment, is to avoid experiencing the meaningless of a life without faith. Such an effort is self-deification and ignores the connectedness of each person with one another and with creation. It is the birthplace of desire and it is natural to human beings. Only when we become spirit and open our eyes to reality can we overcome desire.

This misguided effort to become meaningful is impotent because of mortality, bringing the eternal into the temporal through acts of love is to bring God into the world and such echoes into eternity. Human beings cannot escape suffering, they either harden their hearts to it, or recognize that suffering has meaning because God is watching, because God cares about how we live in relation to one another. Ultimately we do not possess life in ourselves; life is a gift from God.

Blindness is healed when eyes are opened. Love is the healing salve that mediates healing to the fearful; everyone is afraid and everyone wants to be loved. Love is irrational, love is self-sacrificing, love is not selfish and offers mercy to all. The love of God flows through a life, a person, whose belief in the goodness of God is supported by a conviction that opens the heart of the blind who long to see.

Face to Face

Standing in Heaven

He needed me
When I found him he was crushed by the weight of reality
His irreducible love, his indomitable hope, had led him
to the precipice of the lost

He invited me to come
He had passed through death's portal and never
relinquished the burden he carried
"Follow me" I heard him say

I chose to come and see
My questions were outweighed by his call, by his way of living
A power gripped my soul and held me captive to a dream

I'm standing in heaven
I chose to continually remain waiting letting others pass ahead
There was one who stood with me

I beheld him face to face

For we see in a mirror, dimly, but then we will see face to face For now I know only in part; then I will know fully, even as I have been fully known. And now faith, hope, and love abide, these three; and the greatest of these is love

First Cor 13:12-13

Facing God

To stand face to face with another is the defining encounter for knowing, for experiencing the spiritual dynamics of relationship. Face to face there is the potential for intimacy, when eyes speak and the intricate movements of the face communicate, when words are defined by inflections in the voice, and body language incorporates the entire person. Face to face is the call to embrace the person of the other who bears the image of God.

Beholding another face to face is a place of equality; if it is not then the encounter is not *face to face*. Without equality the dynamics of the encounter are disrupted by powers that separate one from another. Vulnerability is the essential openness for insuring a truly face to face experience with another. In the man Jesus we can see God face to face, it is in the Lord Jesus Christ that we see God join the creation to experience living as a human being. His continuing existence as a human being is where the *one* who is uniquely Son of God lifts us to learn how to find the invisible, ineffable, God in the human family.

Through the use of poetry, Paul the apostle expressed belief in a time of human and divine encounter when the vulnerability of humanity before the Lord is matched with the vulnerability of God. God's vulnerability is an irreducible love, a love that enters the depths of creaturely difference to lift us up from the earth (ground) to become children of God.

There is no exchange or loss of power, rather there is the knowing of God as the divine lover, the relational redeeming creator who makes inviolable promises to his creatures; the surety of life resident in the source of life, the one God. This knowing eradicates the creature's desire for surpassing the limits of knowing, a limit placed upon us as like, but other than, God.

This moment is the kiss of marriage, the intimacy of humanity incorporated into the Spirit of God. In Christ, humanity learns to live and not reach for fruit beyond the limits

Humanity's perception of the voice of God will have moved from prohibition to 'God our Father'.

of the creature's existence, an existence defined by the wisdom of God. The inward voice of human intellect seeking to explore regions beyond the structures of reality will turn from the prohibited tree and see innumerable trees in the garden of life, each rich with the fruit of life.

Beholding the Lord, the lowly man, the exalted Christ, the patience of eternity calling us ever forward into life, is not a single moment but a constant reality, a spiritual revelation as we are held in the being (Spirit) of God. Hiding and absence are words no longer descriptive of the divine-human relationship. We will know the Lord; all of us, and hierarchical structures of relationship will fade into harmonious creativity.

In Jesus Christ the Lord, part of what it means to be God is to be human. Humanity is incorporated into the being of God and this is an unchangeable reality. In the beginning of scripture we learn that one human being is an incomplete creation; God created us to be many. Jesus is Lord because he is the word, the wisdom of God incarnate, the one who is before all things. Jesus is Lord because he earned this exalted title as the one who conquered all that inhibits human beings from being temples for God.

Face to face we shall behold the one whose mercy endures forever. Face to face we are welcome at the table of God where life is the sustaining food and drink. Face to face the vulnerability of God humbles the children of God

Tell Me a Story

When Storytellers Rule the World
'I' am a story
From the highest heaven he watches
Leaning forward he waits

The drama of history has captured me as one among many
Defined by particularity
At risk to chance

My freedom to choose is always only a will away
Bound by reality
Equipped to defy reality

Now I hear his call
To change the world is simply to be
The courage to be is the faith of a saint

Today 'I' write my own story
a story infused with all the pain of the present
a story untold, never lived before
a story of peace in a land of war

He is my father and 'I' am living his dream
My story has eternal meaning
I am a child of God

But there are also many other things that Jesus did; if every one of them were written down, I suppose that the world itself could not contain the books that would be written.

John 21:25

Tell Me a Story

An omniscient narrator, an unknown author, evidence of editorial work by another, or of sources utilized by a compiler, yet none of these characters are capable of determining with certainty that their reader will ascribe to their intended meaning. Every contributor to, or editor of the biblical text is a guide within a larger framework of the history that has brought the reader to hear their story.

Stories circumvent questions, delay answers, and cloud certainty, yet they ignite imagination, invite critique, and seal their mark on the soul with a power unseen. Stories carry spirit and appeal to spirit. A story has power to change the one who hears and the one who hears has the power to change a story through their uniqueness.

We bring ourselves to the text. This being said, the bible is only as good as the person reading it. The cry for a clean heart is a cry for ears to hear. The task is to hear the voice of God amidst the infusion of humanity's perceptions in a story of both God and humanity.

Christianity cannot grow stagnant if it remains as story, as a living witness to the dynamics of revelation in a people, in a person and in history. Ceremonies attempt to seal a story, but a story can be told in a multitude of

Once your story is told it slips from your hands into the life of another.

ways and defy the institutional drudgery of a ceremony. Stories are like God, like Spirit, they cannot be confined and controlled.

The metanarrative of scripture is an uncontainable story. The error of classical theology and church tradition has been to confine the story to the control of an institution rather than to the lived witness of a people.

In the present age the academy has privileged itself as the interpreter of scripture based upon the arrogance of intellectual technique and privileged access to learning and information. However, without a story, without a life lived in conjunction with God's presence among the poor and oppressed then interpretation becomes about maintaining power rather than serving others. The tedious repetition of academic effort apart from the face-to-face encounter with God among the people is vanity (hevel).

So, tell me a story of grace, a story of justice, a story of liberation, a story of unbound love, of sacrifice and joy. Tell me a story of hope against hope, of dramatic personal challenge, of change and growth into the image of God in Christ Jesus. Tell me a story where people learn to hear the voice of God and see *thy kingdom come* in the present, where people enter the rest of heaven in the hell of the present. Tell me a human story infused with the life of God.

Prophetic Denunciation

When Prophets Weep

Broken beneath the weight of divine pathos
Longing for eternity
Holding onto the present
Speech alone releases the load

Unable to release his own humanity
Or escape the God who will not let him go
He Speaks

Overwhelmed
His vision of humanity belongs to God
There is no hiding

Laid at the gate of a globalized world are the children of Lazarus
Capitalism displays contempt for life
Empire is indicative of God's absence
There is no hiding

Militarism belongs to those who crucify the innocent
God's army is disrobed
Bearing words for weapons
There is no hiding

The consumption of the gods of the earth
has sent God's children to scavenge refuse
The warring of the god's of the earth
threatens all of humanity

They ignore their mortality
There is no hiding
when Prophets speak

Do not trust in these deceptive words: "This is the temple of the LORD, the temple of the LORD, the temple of the LORD."

Jer 7:4

When Prophets Speak

Prophetic denunciation is an uncompromising view on reality. It is expressed through Spirit driven pathos embodied in a human life, a life formed for speaking truth to power. It is the formation of the prophetic soul under the hand of God that produces a persona whose perception of truth is matched with speech that brings the voice of God into the world as denouncement.

Prophetic denunciation is more than correction or ethical discernment; it is an unquestionable charge, a truth that of its own

> *Prophetic denunciation makes each human being responsible for their relationship to the powers.*

power denotes guilt. It is the heart of God exposed in the life and flesh of the speaker. It is a demand for change regardless of the institutional structures that justify systemic oppression through ideology and law.

Prophetic denouncement is not gloom and doom preaching, it is not interested in the end of the world but the transformation of the present. As an activity it is dangerous and exposes the speaker or writer to the animus of the powerful. Prophetic denouncement is often the language of the martyr. Prophetic denouncement is the most potent form of speech that is accomplished on behalf of the powerless.

In the *scandalon* of the cross we know that an innocent victim was put to death, we know that victim to have been the Son of God. The scandal of the present is the ongoing crucifixion of the poor and oppressed masses of people across the earth, vic-

> *To ignore the poor, the uneducated, the trafficked, is to live in contempt for both God and Humanity.*

tims to imperialism, to democratic capitalism, they scavenge dumpsites, they sell their bodies, they are shut out from the wealth of the earth held by a few.

A society that celebrates the wealthy and does not view their excessive lifestyles as deplorable is a society in need of prophetic denunciation. A church that does not come alongside the poor but names international fellowship with the churches of wealthier nations as missions is in need of prophetic denunciation.

A Church that allows for, or promotes, the association of Christian faith with their nation's militarism is a church in need of prophetic denunciation. A Church that takes money from poor widows in the name of *tithing* is in need of prophetic denunciation.

"... *neither shall they learn war anymore*" *is not simply prophetic hope for the future, it is indicative of Christian practice for the present.*

Praying to God our father *thy kingdom come* is to receive the reign of God in the present by living the will of God. It is God's will that we bring the poor down from the cross.

Wealth Mobility and Christian Mission

Bearing the Weight of the Poor

I carry them with me always
Visions of their smiles haunt me

Blackness marks the sickness that consumes their flesh,
their ears, their nose their fingers, their legs
I saw them at Nago
The stench, the smile, the humanity being ate alive

I carry them with me always
I weep because they are treated as less than animals

Clawing at the refuse of the city
with a sharp hooked rod
a hungry human being eats food from the smoldering dump
a child who will never learn to read
a child enduring boils and flies

I carry him with me always
I never gave him enough

a man with a board on coasters using his
gloved hands to push his self along
reaching up he asks for a coin
looking down I empty my pocket

I carry her with me always
She could have been a girl in my High School

Her youth and beauty fade each year
She remembers her children shot in a clash between warring factions
Her son by an unknown wretch holds her hand
She is for sale nightly
a numbered tag replaces her name

I carry them with me always
Their fragile lives bring tears to my eyes

Little children with their hands held out
Playing with tires
Feet without shoes
Laughing at their growling stomach

I carry them with me always
I see the emptiness in their souls

A cupped hand, a swelled pocket, floating eyes
With sleight of hand they sniff quickly
Glue eats their brains
Stunts their growth
They chose to escape an uninhabitable world

I carry her with me always
She haunts my dreams

Unkempt hair, a tattered dress,
an exhausted child nursing at her dry breast
My alms could not bring her smile

I carry them all and many more
They have become a part of my soul
They are the reason I speak
They are the reason I don't like your hiding place called church

Then he will answer them, "Truly I tell you, just as you did not do it to one of the least of these, you did not do it to me."

Matt 25:45

Mobility and Crossing Borders

The defining sign of a wealthy society and a powerful nation is the mobility of its citizens. The power of a blue passport, the security of surplus, enable a people in search of identity, to find their identity in contrast to the lack in the life of others. Mobility has become a defining rite of American identity; for both the elderly and the youth of the U.S.

For the elderly who remember when only the very rich, long term missionaries, and members of the military experienced travelling overseas, the cruise or touring vacation is a sign of status, of arriving at a place of achievement from the hardships of their youth. For the youth of the U.S. travelling overseas is a rite of passage into adulthood, it is the adventure that provides a story for youth's lack of experience.

The voyeurism of our image driven culture is easily transferred over into a trip abroad. The power of mobility, of the empire's passport, and the detachment of a soul in search of identity, all contribute to the alien status of U.S. citizens travelling overseas. The separation, the distance of the U.S. citizen from the people, the ingrained ideology of 'exceptionalism' all produce the phenomenon of group trips where the travellers do not connect with the people, culture, or even the reality of difference, when in another country.

Of course the presence of U.S. staples like fast food corporations, the movie industry, and U.S. military presence permeating the world provide the American traveller with the familiarity of home, the power of their economics, the influence of their culture; an American can always find someone who speaks English!

Crossing Borders

The airline industry has provided unprecedented mobility for international global travel. When entering a nation where poverty abounds Christians must avoid two manners of living in relation to the poor. First, is to ignore them and enjoy the developed tourist locations. Second, is to become merely a voyeur, guilty of seeing and forgetting.

The first scriptural 'rule' or ethic for crossing a border is depicted in the ceremonial placement of some stones found in the story of Jacob and Laban. Abraham and Lot separated before violence broke out between an uncle and nephew's clan. Likewise Jacob and Laban separate to avoid violence between the two family 'houses' of Jacob and Laban. The agreement is about treatment of Laban's daughters and that the boundary markers remind one another that they will not cross to cause the other harm.

In the covenant between Jacob and Laban are two instructive rules for international relations. First, is in the event that a person marries a spouse from another country, the spouse (women in particular) is to be treated as an equal and not a foreigner. Further the covenant agreement teaches us that we do not cross boundaries to harm the people on the other side.

These two 'rules' from the stories of scripture serve as behavioral models for both nation states and individual persons. Whether a person *hides* by visiting only the tourist sites, or like a voyeur captures images of the poor and does not aid them, they are guilty of ignoring the poor.

Bringing God into the World

I often state that ignoring the poor is contempt for both humanity and God. I think this is the intent behind Jesus teaching in the gospel about not helping the poor and oppressed.

> *Then he will answer them,*
> *'Truly I tell you, just as you did not do*
> *it to one of the least of these,*
> *you did not do it to me".*
>
> *Matt 25:45*

Jesus is the human embodiment of God (incarnation), so ignoring the poor is an act against both humanity and God; this is so because ignoring the poor is to ignore Jesus. The healing of the world lies in the concerted effort of all humanity to end poverty. It is an act that brings the life of God, the Spirit of God, the Christ into the world.

The activity of ending poverty as a people is an activity for nation states. This is made clear in Matthew 25 when Jesus judges the nations based upon their care for the poor. For this reason it is legitimate prophetic activity to bring the nation state into account for all systemic structures that produce wealth at the expense, the suffering, (even the crucifixion) of the poor. If the state can be held responsible for ending systemic structures that cause poverty, how much more shall the people of God and the institution called *church* be emphatic about the right of the poor and needy to her wealth? Meaning, all economic decisions are subject to God's love and care for the poor.

All of my claims express the truth that loving God is inseparable from loving your neighbor; the victim of injustice on the side of the road.

Living in the Way

The Way of the Saint

Those exemplary souls
Their lives cause us to see God
They are Jesus to the world

Obstinate, Independent, Immovable
Living in the way
Their foreignness disrupts our world

They have traversed the chasm from fear to love
Their fear is lost in love's grip
Love is their call
Relieving suffering is love's abode
God is there

They walk with God
They walk with the forgotten of the earth
They walk in opposition to the politics of profit
They walk like Jesus

Justice is their creed
God their confession
A singular voice enters their ears

They build a legacy of words
a memory of exceptional living
Their memory is a story without monuments

They build humanity
In the likeness of God

the Son of Man has come eating and drinking, and you say, "Look,
a glutton and a drunkard, a friend of tax collectors and sinners!"

Luke 7:34

Living the Way

In the biblical narrative the pursuit of how we are to live as hu-
man beings is plagued by our failings to live in accordance with
the intention and desire of our creator, our God. It is immediately
apparent that our propensity to violence, brought on by desire,
set us on a course from which we have failed to learn how to end
violence. We do violence to ourselves when fulfilling our desire to
reach beyond our creatureliness, or by not reaching for God. We
do violence to others out of misplaced desire and rivalries; these
acts of violence are willful, violate our moral conscience, spread
the presence of death throughout reality and place us outside the
way of God for humanity.

Fear of the Lord is the beginning of wisdom, the beginning
point for learning the way. We learn to love God as we grow in
knowledge of God's goodness, God's holiness. It is the discerning
of God's voice in the creation that moves faith further along to a
place of relationship. The chasm between fear and love is the place
of journey that challenges to live in the way.

The way of God is always a way that requires following. We
are to follow the Lord. Moses the man who spoke face to face
with God asks to be shown the ways of God. He is sheltered in a
crevice and during his revelation he sees only the back of God as
God passes by him and moves away. Although Moses was likely
provided insight and revelation into the ways of God, the pictur-
esque moment reveals that the revelation is ongoing and requires

following; there are no concrete rules to insure one is following; only the ongoing role as follower. Paul understands his own exemplary role and declares it is good to follow him as he follows the Lord. The religious leader whether prophet or apostle is also a follower, someone who is still learning, on the adventurous road where God and humanity walk together.

In John's gospel, Jesus knew himself to be the embodiment of truth, life and *the way*. The three are inseparable; one is inclusive of the others, and of Jesus. In effect, Jesus is the definition for experiencing and living wholeness as a human being (son of man), of living out the image of God borne by humanity. Jesus is nothing like David the murderous nation builder. Jesus does not want to be king of a nation state. Jesus is Lord and desires a 'bride' a 'people' who can be children of God.

The covenant formula 'I will be their God and they shall be my people' is the refrain of God's salvific work in humanity. The people of God do not require the constructs of a nation state in order to live

God never desired a nation state; God's desire has always been for a people.

in the way of Jesus. We are all called to be Saints.

Christian Resistance

World Creators

Alone we dream
Together we create reality
The hope for newness to enter the world rests in God's children
Resistance is a Christian posture

The culture calls—resist
The state calls—resist
Society calls—resist
God calls—follow

Sages and prophets
Martyrs for a dream
Leaving stories, words, for another generation
Theologians of hope and challenge

Rivalries all around
Nation states all so proud
Ever beating the drum of war
They are all wrong, none are right

America
a place where liberty is only a statue
America
a place where excess is god
America
a place where war is a business
America
an empire where democracy is a myth

God Bless
Our children to resist
not with weapons or fists
but with wisdom and one another
Freedom of speech is impotent without freedom of thought

But Peter and the apostles answered, "We must obey God rather than any human authority."

Acts 5:29

Christian Resistance

Christian resistance is the uncompromising position of a believer determined to remain within the reign of God and accept their status as an alien. A Christian resistor is a person whose moral and ethical life is understood to be relevant to all parts of life. A Christian resistor is one who resists evil with good. Christian resistance is nonviolent and uses informed theological speech to promote peace and merciful justice in a world where violence is legitimized. Christian resistance initially functions through non-cooperation with unjust powers. Christian resistance is a spiritual discipline and practice.

Although Christian resistance is often noted in a few exemplary persons, it is the collective effort of the Christian community that makes possible the exemplary leaders status. Christian resistance is a community-based lifestyle rooted in faith and belief in the resurrection.

I think the most important power to resist in the present is the recruitment of children and young people for military service. To resist this power of the state, a power sustained through the idols of nationalism and militarism, is imperative. If it is not resisted

22

then it is easily tolerated. A community that remains isolated from the larger society can hold values consistent with resistance yet fail to impact society directly. However if a community of people actively work within society and touch the lives of others through their work and teaching, said community will be subject to the animus of proud patriots.

The reason I consider this particular form of resistance an immediate need and imperative is because behind the recruitment of America's youth is the older generations belief in the idea of American exceptionalism. This self-righteous acclamation is the impetus of belief that sustains the idols of nationalism and militarism. The participation of the evangelical movement in these idols requires a response of rebuke from all Christians of faith and courage. Christianity is not about being 'nice' as some suppose and peddle their brand of therapeutic preaching.

> The greatest danger to Christianity is, I contend, not heresies, not heterodoxies, not atheists, not profane secularism - no, but the kind of orthodoxy which is cordial drivel, mediocrity served up sweet. There is nothing that so insidiously displaces the majestic as cordiality.
>
> —Soren Kierkegaard

Unfortunately, freedom of speech is non-existent when the populace is fodder to the state propagandists. The blinding power of pride expressed in the doctrine of American Exceptionalism has commandeered the voice of god in much of the evangelical community. Persons who speak and challenge American Exceptionalism as immoral or un-Christian are excluded from long standing evangelical institutions.

Call of the Wild

Untamable

God laughs and refuses domestication
His will, inscrutable to the keepers of civility
His ethic, ever open, ever alive
Leviathan he mocks

The call of the wild can be held in the soul
It rests at peace with the natural world
It is courageous in the face of those who neuter humanity
In God it breaks forth to heal the status quo
It is the faith of a Sparrow

The unified voice of cultural civility conceals its crimes with a smile
Unable to change
Standing in the place of self-justifying power
Demanding conformation

God calls forth the wild, the untamable,
the suffering servant of boldness
living out likeness and image

The cutting power of difference embodied in flesh that speaks
His freedom is his undoing in the world below
Like thunder, like lightning, his life can never be forgotten

Defying keepers of culture
he challenged civility's norms,
empire's power, and religion's institutionalized authority
It is true,
he opened his arms and embraced the entire world

God's servants
with a taste of the wild
hold their individuality as inviolable
Long for the unification of Christ's body
Refuse social neutering
Reject culture as determinative for faith›s expressions

Today's renegades are tomorrow's martyrs
Their lives, like a voice from the wilderness, cannot be forgotten
The keepers of culture seek to neuter their memory
So they write
Others write about them

They live on in the wild souls of another generation
They learn to be like Jesus

Now John wore clothing of camel's hair with a leather belt around his waist, and his food was locusts and wild honey.

Matt 3:4

Call of the Wild

As creatures of flesh capable of becoming *spirit* we live in a world where the wild facets of nature and its creatures is ever near. In all of us rests a little wildness. The nature of the civilization of power is a denial of the goodness to be found in wildness. It is not the childish wildness of a bohemian, or of unrestrained animal instincts, that I refer to. Rather, it is the adventurous love for life arrested by boldness for living that is a witness to the indomitable

Spirit of Jesus; a witness that defies the systemic structures of evil in societal constructs.

The God speeches in Job offer us contemplation on the wildness of God. In these speeches God enjoys the wild creatures, cares for the wild creatures and rules over all that is wild. Job would civilize God and bring him into the court of human understanding, but he cannot.

This love of the wild can be seen in some of the characters God uses. My initial favorite is the wild man Elijah. In spite of his violence God uses Elijah, and his faith is as wild as his person. Elijah failed to learn from Obadiah or the widow. His failure to learn to think critically about the world resulted in his ominous death by the chariots of Israel.

Jeremiah is an educated, civilized man; he learns that the wild unpredictable meaning of, "Do not be afraid of them, for I am with you to deliver you, says the Lord" does not allow for cultural civility. Jeremiah is a disturber of the peace, a traitor of the state, an uncivilized orator of religious critique; he shatters the religio-culutral symbolic world of his age. His only friend is a man named Baruch who records his words, he must stand alone against his culture, and do so apart from his family's desire for him to be a supporter of normalcy.

Jesus' first supporter is a wild man who lives as an indomitable individual. Jesus would refer to John as one who had arrived at a measure of greatness not to be compared with others.

Jesus lives out a model for incorporating the goodness of wildness with the goodness of humanity. Jesus resists the powers that domesticate humanity like neutered animals. Jesus lives out a model for humanity that rests with God and the world in which we live.

All that has been done in the name of civilization has been accomplished in *Civilization is built upon the unethical control of nature and human beings.* disjunction with the natural world and the flourishing of all. Civilization is a system of sacrifice where progress requires the death and suffering of others. Christianity seeks new wine skins.

The Moment

Today I Die

I must stand
I will not be moved
My death will speak innumerable words

My life has become a beacon of peace
The world watches
A lone soul against a war machine

My only defense is to be non-violent
My death will denounce violence
I am sheep for slaughter

The blood of my brothers and sisters will not release me
Yesterday they were slaughtered
But today I die

While they were stoning Stephen, he prayed, "Lord Jesus, receive my spirit."

Acts 7:59

Today I Die

This poem is written in memory of *tank man*, who withstood a line of tanks in Tiananmen Square on June 5th 1989. The Chinese army had crushed the pro-democracy movement the night before. After halting the line of tanks, for a moment, the man spoke to a crewmember in the tank through the gunner's hatch. The man's identity and whether he lived or died is unknown. He was pulled away by a couple of persons to enter the annals of history as a representative of the human spirit in the face of military power turned upon its own people.

Every military trains its personnel in such a way that they can be used to maintain national order even if they must kill their citizens, their own countrymen. In this respect the *military cult* is the most powerful brainwashing institution ever devised in the name of governing. In the U.S. the incident at Kent State remains a reminder of this reality for those who think their children are ethically superior to military training. The military cult is a religious brotherhood built on myths of the divine warrior and the honorable death of sacrifice on behalf of national identity.

The religious element that seduces is the idol of nationalism. As an idol, the nation state is the ultimate good and the order of the state requires the sacrifice of self (or your children) in an act of honor. It is no small task to turn men into mass killers. It takes a culture of violence, an ideology that exalts the warrior as an expression of divinity. This is clearly seen in the belief that some men are warriors by nature (created to be warriors), this lie is rooted in the religion of Platonism. Plato›s warrior class is an ideology taught throughout the west from prep schools to West Point.

There can never be a Christian nation, only a Christian people. The scripture makes it clear that the state commandeers the voice of God for its own use. The state makes itself the ultimate power in the lives of its citizens and because it cannot compete with religious conviction, simply aligns itself with the religion(s) of the populace. The syncretism of religion and state produces the idol of nationalism.

The unknown man who withstood a line of tanks in Tiananmen Square is like the warrior Paul presents in Ephesians chapter six. He is without armor, without a uniform, without offensive or defensive weapons, he is stripped of all that identifies a warrior. Yet he demonstrated beyond any soldier what it is to be a man, a human being.

Victims of Abuse

Unwanted

Captured in a rolling landslide of temporal suffering
Wondering where the innocence of my own person became irretrievable
A scapegoat, a victim, an object of rejection

Longing to shout, to be heard, to contribute to humanity
Knowing, seeing, hearing, the voice of the Lord
Gripped in soul, with thoughts flowing faster than time

Believing in a way brightly lit
Walking along crippled and slow, steady and weak, sure footed of
necessity
Comforted by truth speaking people
Disturbed by blindness

There is one who calls me, I reply, "Here am I"
Perhaps that is enough
Perhaps it is not

Deliver me O Lord from the silence of separation
From the silence of obscurity
Toss me into the flurries of humanity one more time
I will be faithful to speak the truth
Hear O Lord while I am still alive

He was despised and rejected by others; a man of suffering and acquainted with infirmity; and as one from whom others hide their faces he was despised, and we held him of no account.

Isa 53:3

Exclusion and Inclusion

The politics of exclusion exists in both church and society. We are all victims of sin before we are perpetrators and often those in power do not see their own sin but only the erring of another. Perhaps no other person in history has communicated the phenomenon of communal scapegoating as well as Rene Girard.

The tensions of chaotic forces in culture, relationships, expectations, build to a crisis moment that requires a person upon whom all the tension can fall. The tension exists in a multitude of unresolved words, misinterpreted glances, institutional challenges; this tension in existence is alive like a legion of demons. The person upon whom the power falls is often different than the rest, perhaps older, a physical defect, a bearer of difference that conflicts with the communal dynamic.

It is the sad story of humanity that we often sacrifice the finest among us for the sake of peace and always because love has failed. In the church this phenomenon of scapegoating has caused harm to many. A victim of social scapegoating is in need of acceptance. These souls carry with them hope for resurrection in the now, to see life again after severe emotional suffering. In the thought of Miraslov Volf, exclusion is healed only by embrace, by reconciliation. In the gospel the offering of embrace often comes from the abused one. Only love can produce such an outcome, nonetheless there must be acceptance for there to be reconciliation.

Most modern persons fail to recognize the group *spirit* that grips families, institutions, crowds, and churches. This parasitical power captures the judgment of everyone without the awareness that exclusion is most often not born of the sin of the excluded. Rather, it is in the tension of change, of challenge, that groups isolate by naming a single person as unacceptable. Once this process is set in motion naming the person's behavior becomes an authorized form of gossip. Slowly the assassination of the person's character comes under the kind of scrutiny that no individual could escape.

On a larger scale, when entire groups of people experience exclusion, it is often through the evil of racism or nationalism. As human beings we either give ourselves to the *spirit of Christ* or we generate an anti-Christ group spirit. Anti-Christ in contrast to the reality that only 'in Christ' can humanity fulfill her calling to become children of God. Whenever people fulfill the *spirit of Christ* in behavior and beliefs they function in accordance with God's desire for humanity, whether they have been told about Jesus or not.

Anti-Christ is the corporate, or group *spirit,* of humanity. Exclusion is the sign of its presence. Inclusion, forgiveness, patience, grace, and love halt the practice of exclusion. In Christ the evil of exclusion should not occur and if it does, it can be healed. Unfortunately we refuse to learn enough about ourselves to avoid the sin of excluding.

Go with Me

I Will Be With You

I will be with you
If
I will be with you
but perhaps you will not recognize me

I will be with you
You will know this afterward
Had I not been
The darkness would have crushed you

I will be with you
Loving you with moments of peace
Leaving you with gifts that make you more than dirt

I will be with you
when you surrender to reality
and when you fight

I will be with you
when all reason has vanished
I will be your reason

I will be with you
when everyone leaves you
Learning to love when love is lost
I will love with you

I will be with you when they persecute you
they persecute me
we will suffer together

I will be with you
when time and death
steal your strength
and take your dreams

I will be with you
at your last breath
I will breathe you in to myself
I will never lose you
I am with you

Do not be afraid of them,
for I am with you to deliver you,
says the Lord

Jer. 1:8

Go with Me

I have been fascinated with God's statement to Jeremiah in his call narrative since the day I read it (Jeremiah 1:8).

God's manner of being with Jeremiah is not determinative for success and a life filled with joy. Jeremiah will endure exclusion, be told to remain a single man, suffer torture, experience his own family seeking to take his life, be arrested for activity equivalent to treason, and in all this, God was with him.

I suggest that the presence of God that accompanied Jeremiah is displayed in his resilience to recover from humiliation, persecution, and social rejection. Jeremiah's ministry is incompatible with modern concepts of social intelligence and success. Jeremiah is not a team player. He is a man who stands alone, burning with passion for truth, and the entrance of God into the affairs of his world.

His genius is his dismantling of a socio-religious culture whose symbols have lost their meaning. He imagines a world where a return to those symbols is annulled. Jeremiah pushes forward the faith of his people's history and soul towards the God who is the object of their faith. Jeremiah liberates the people of God to live their faith within the confines of empire. Jeremiah's work does more to form the identity of *Israel* than Joshua's. Jewish identity has survived empires, genocidal efforts, and global dispersion.

So, when Paul writes that we can do all things through Christ, the 'all things' is the mess that is in the world, the mess we must rise above as God's children. From the words of a wise old Sunday school teacher we learn that the best we can do is learn to love our way through the mess.

The Archetypal Strongman

Samson the Archetype

Illiterate reading like children
Making legends of anti-heroes
Delighting in tales of unrestrained Man

Making movies, writing books, exalting the fool
a religion that has lost its way

Strength without insight
Virility wasted on Instinct
a people
Ethically blinded by aesthetics
lost to a god of self-destruction

The strongman honors no vows
His selfishness that of a spoiled son
A wasted life reduced to pulsating muscles
A living symbol of Phallicism

Uneducated refusing wisdom, refusing his mother
He feeds upon death
Honey from carcasses
Water from rotten marrow of a bone

A man who cannot discern the difference between God and adrenaline
His will defeated by a porn-queen
His addiction blinds him, binds him, he dies

Blind and bound in the temple of a god
A symbol like his people
a death self inflicted

When he awoke from his sleep, he thought, "I will go out as at other times, and shake myself free." But he did not know that the LORD had left him.

Judg 16:20

Reading the Samson Story

The story of Samson has long been read in a romanticized way that ignores all morality and wisdom. Samson is an archetype, a symbol; he is Israel during the time of the Judges when males lost all regard for females, for life.

His unnamed mother was called to be, and remained, a Nazarite throughout her life. She spoke wisdom and discerned the voice of God. His father rejected his mother's wisdom for his own vision of male grandeur. Manoah celebrated and coddled Samson's gladiator like prowess.

Samson judged no one, delivered no one, caused uncontrollable wild fires, slaughtered young men for a wager, loved a seductress and lost his life to his addiction. His legend is the tale of a violent man in a book that celebrates violent men, a book that ends in tribal genocide, the killing of their own brothers, the murdering of non-violent people, the trafficking of their women and then organized kidnapping of another group of women.

Christian America is not unlike Israel, is not unlike Samson. She is illiterate and unable to read her scriptures with a moral conscience. She, exalts the gladiator and celebrates the insatiable man and the seductress, she is blind. The Samson story is written to expose Israel›s errant ways, to symbolize her society in a perennial archetype - the Strongman.

The way of wisdom is to provide equal voice to males and females in society. The way of wisdom is to live morally, develop your mind over your body and restrain sexual desire to the male female relationship under a promise. The way of wisdom is a nonviolent way because it does no damage to the image of God in the human.

Wrestling and Identity

Esau, Self and God

Wrestling from the womb
The stronger the weaker
Manly man Mama's boy
A lifelong rivalry

Favored by father
Favored by mother
Divided by nature
Divided by family

Man hunger, fierce independence
An inappropriate deal
Sealed with deceit

Anger rages
Run Jacob run

A peaceful Bedouin
returns home
A tribal chieftain
Ready to wrestle

Little twin hides on the other side of the river
His wealth and love goes before him

His wild ass of a brother
Older seasoned
Comes to play
To learn if little twin has changed

Jacob wrestled self, his brother, and God
Esau's strength, Jacob's tenacity, leaves a limp
Reconciled, in Esau, Jacob beholds the face of God

Jacob said, "No, please; if I find favor with you, then accept my present from my hand; for truly to see your face is like seeing the face of God—since you have received me with such favor."

Gen 33:10

Wrestling

The lifelong rivalry of a perennial wrestling match between the twin brothers culminates in a nightlong struggle. Literarily, Jacob's partner in this nightlong match cannot be limited to one interpretive reading. Jacob wrestles with his self. He has been a trickster; he has used deceit and wisdom to survive. He learned to use his mind rather than a stone (like Cain). He became a breeder of animals to overcome his family's practice of greed and treachery.

Now, with all his life surrendered to his brother he confronts self, Esau, and God in a single night of travail. It is completely consistent with the character of Esau to sneak across the river in the middle of the night to learn whether little brother has changed or is still an under developed deceiver. Jacob seeks only blessing and refuses to release his opponent.

God joins in the struggle between the two brothers. Esau remains powerful and hurt. Jacob is changed and peace is more important than stuff. God wants reconciliation, forgiveness. Esau gets his vengeance and Jacob finally comes to terms with the truth, although he walks away with a limp, forgiveness must win the day, reconciliation between brothers is the realm of God.

The Problem of Evil

Systemic Structures of Evil

I have solved the problem of evil
Said no one ever
There was no devil in the garden
Evil was born a parasite
Dependent upon humanity

A good God
The presence of evil
Evil prevails when good souls do nothing

It was Hitler's nationalism
It was Luther's anti-Semitism
It was a Church without prophetic Martyrs

Satan cannot cast out Satan
Who will bind the Strongman?
There is one who binds
One who speaks

Illiteracy is not the inability to read
it is the inability to hear
Hearing isn't reading
it is living

Another empire on the verge of collapse
Another demagogue longing to rise
Another theologian blind in the mirror
Another church without martyrs

Structures of evil deeply engrained
A world in crisis
Whispers of religious
hissing for apocalyptic mushrooms

When war is a business that rapes the world,
terror rises, born of the same spirit
Satan cannot cast out Satan

God and Guns
an incompatible duo
gods and Guns
Idolatrous

Martyrs stand and resist the world
Idolaters do not know what to resist
Materialism, Militarism, and Nationalism
The unholy trinity of idolatry

It would seem that in America
There ain't no Christians no mo

[7] And will not God grant justice to his chosen ones who cry to him day and night? Will he delay long in helping them? [8] I tell you, he will quickly grant justice to them. And yet, when the Son of Man comes, will he find faith on earth?"

Luke 18:7-8

The Prophetic Martyr as Sentinel against Idolatry

The prophetic martyr possesses a sensitivity that resists evil in its earliest manifestation. Such a person possesses a consistency in matters of human affairs, a certain relentless opposition to all that would inhibit justice and righteousness. The prophetic martyr is first a non-compromising soul.

> *The writings of prophetic martyrs are the soul of Christian history.*

It is vital that Christianity acknowledges these martyrs and celebrates their lives. They teach us to walk with God; they live as citizens of heaven. They are the exemplars of faith that provide for us a model consistent with the life of Jesus.

The personification of evil is always a move away from acknowledging the inter-related culpability of humanity, the systemic structures of evil in society, culture, and politics. The most immediate and threatening devil is always the one in the mirror. Calls to abolish evil as an incurable malignancy resonate with the hissing of destruction seen in a mushroom cloud.

The illiteracy of evangelical Christianity culminates in an allegiance to the state that is irreconcilable with our faith. At this point in history the volatile environment of the present is subject to nationalism because the church has lost the potency of the prophetic word. Christianity has become impotent.

The teaching of two kingdoms that legitimizes temporal powers as instruments of God in the present is particularly injurious to Christian faith. It calls for duplicity in faith, duplicity in human behavior; it misunderstands the call of God. The Christian position in relation to the state is tolerance and the arena of political engagement is resistance of all injustice.

Facing Reality

Facing and Rejecting Reality

Awareness begins
human reality
an unseen power living in each one
an outward structure formed flawed

Burden touches the soul
distaste for suffering
rottenness in reality

Culpability questions
seeks healing
rejects reality
faces reality

Facing reality wisdom begins creating
Imagination forms a new reality
Saints live in an unseen world
the reality of God
we can change the world

Accepting mortality
Living as though death is impotent
Spiritual intelligence subverts reality

Tolerating powers
Forming a new reality
Returning to the garden
Walking with the voice of God
One day blood cries will be heard no more

and free those who all their lives were held in slavery by the fear of death.

Heb 2:15

Spiritual Intelligence

Spiritual intelligence is to face reality from the position of heaven, with the vision of God. It is not a delusional view but one of revelatory clarity. Spiritual intelligence recognizes the temporary powers as subject to the power of the gospel; a gospel of good news wherein God is determined to redeem humanity in the present through the faith of those who know him.

In the eyes of God nothing is hidden. All the devices of wickedness practiced in the halls of power are exposed. Spiritual wickedness in high places isn't about devils resisting angels above the earth! Spiritual wickedness is in government, in corporate offices, in economic institutions, in the weapons business;

The 'giants' of the earth still live in golden towers, with their power they still take women at their whim.

these are the high places where human beings become fodder for the advancement of a few, for temporary power.

The first step to spiritual intelligence is awareness of human complicity for the evil that befalls so many across our world. This awareness is easily achieved for a person exposed to the plight of the poor, if that person has a heart like God's, a heart of compassion and love.

Once the heart is opened to the needs of others and becomes aware of the injustice that destroys their life, then, if, a person begins to carry a burden for the suffering of the poor and oppressed they move forward towards spiritual intelligence. God cares for the poor and suffering of the world. Jesus identified his self and presence to be with the poor inasmuch as when we help the poor we are serving Jesus.

God loves humanity, all of us. A person who knows or is attempting to know God will also love humanity and will be moved to correct the injustices that cause suffering. At this point each of us face our particular culpability for how we respond to the overwhelming need in the world. These: awareness, burden and culpability are the steps to facing reality with our eyes opened.

I am indebted to the prophetic martyr Ignacio Ellacuria for his thoughts on Spiritual Intelligence.

Sin Manifests Evil

The Devil in the Mirror

I look away
I know myself
I've died and been reborn
Still I know myself
I look away

If I stay away from people
I'm okay
I love people
I hate to stay away

My belief in the devil I've resigned to the mirror
A lying reflection
I know myself
I'm not that person

If I nurtured arrogance
I could hide behind a lie
Humility makes me vulnerable
I cannot win

Learning to lose
Avoiding mirrors
These false images surround
Where is truth found?

I looked in the mirror today
I saw millions of people standing in my way

I couldn't find myself amid the myriad of faces
When I saw them all, the devil went away

Masses of souls
All alone
All loved
All afraid of the mirror

I embraced the mirror
I drew it into myself
I'm only human
But I've learned to know the Divine

But one is tempted by one's own desire, then, when that desire has conceived, it gives birth to sin, and that sin, when it is fully grown, gives birth to death.

Jas 1:14-15

Seeing Clearly

Of course, sin is a position before God and not just an act. Sin is also an English word packed with all the meaning provided to it through multiple religious traditions. Sin is also present in complex socio-cultural and political systems. The scripture tells us that the whole world lies in wickedness.

Evil exists in all the damaging acts of sin that have entered the world through human beings. It is a parasitical power roaring like a lion ready to destroy. Evil's

People prefer to believe in an omnipotent devil rather than face their own sin, or their complicity for the state of reality.

most potent power is in the crowd when masses of humanity are captured in agreement over an ideology inconsistent with the Spirit and reign of God.

Luther's acceptance of the two-kingdom theology along with his anti-Semitism was the evil ideology that existed in the German people, in the Lutheran church. The greater evil was the eugenic oriented nationalism that birthed Nazi power.

Denmark's nonviolent approach to Hitler's regime is a story in need of being heard in American Christianity.

We are called to judge ourselves first! We live in a globalized world where the demon of capitalism rapes most of humanity leaving them outside the flourishing life of the earth that belongs to us all. We equate America with the ideals of Christian faith. The truth is you can jump up and down all day and yell at the devil but if you don't recognize the demonic idolatry of your own society, of your own nation, and live out your faith in resistance to the evil in your own immediate environment your just a bunch of hot air.

We are an Empire with military colonizing bases placed across the globe. Our empire supports the excessively, even sinfully wealthy of our nation and the world.

Once the faith is co-opted by the state then the malignancy of nationalism in all its evil possesses the masses. The greatest threat to America is an ineffective church that bows at the idolatrous evils of militarism, materialism and nationalism.

We see clearly in the mirror when we see the faces of the masses of humanity and are moved with compassion to work with God for the healing of the world.

Offence

Look for those who Offend

I am a restless soul
Innocuous spirituality is an empty promise
The offensive rock of speech brings forth water
My soul is ignited with a vision
a dream of the knowledge of God
it offends, it crushes, it creates

To articulate the world to come
The rest of God
Naming the unnamed
Disrobing Clerics
Shaking the pillars of static religion

God's people, Christ's body
Born to be
Bringers of creative reality

Are there Christians anymore?
To find them
Look for those who offend

Look for those who speak a language of peace
Who reject the inevitability of war

Look for those who speak "We are one"
Who trespass ethnicity with love, marriage, children

Look for those who
will die for Christ but not a flag
Look for those who
share with one another until there is no poor among them

Look for those who
reject celebrity but honor servants
Look for those who
educate, clothe and feed the children of Lazarus

Look for those souls who
are uncomfortable with the world as it is,
who live as foreigners in the world.

Look for those who offend
Politics
Patriotism
National Identity
Popular Christianity
Look for those who offend

"Behold, I am laying in Zion y a stone of stumbling, and a rock of offense; zand whoever believes in him will not be a put to shame."

Rom 9:33

The Joy of Offence

It is words that guide us toward truth, that make creation real. It is in the Spirit that words reach beyond their immediacy to enrapture the soul with faith hope and love. Yes, words are like spirit.

The words of Jesus remain offensive to us, even to many of Jesus' followers, both past and present.

God the builder of a temple comprised of human beings has laid the first stone from which the rest of the building will be squared. However this stone seems to be in the way of those who profess to be builders of God's house. This is so because Jesus made the grandeur of a temple to serve only as imagery for a living body of believers. Priests still love to build temples that are dedicated more to their greatness than to the people of God. Where can robed priests or celebrity preachers claim to mediate the presence of God without their temples?

Jesus is a rock of offense, a scandal! It is offensive to the powers who require great buildings to affirm their power that a sandaled itinerant poet, peasant, teacher and prophet would point to himself as the builder of a temple not made with hands. Jesus is announcing a revolution in human relations, a revolution that brings the reign of God into the world, a world where God is King.

Jesus' invited us into a new reality, a reality where human beings live 'in Christ', that is in a harmonious relationship with God and the world. Christian disciples and followers are to be people who live out an imagined world so that it is no longer in the realm of imagination. This activity is offensive to the powers of institutions that are dependent upon injustice and compromise.

There is perhaps no more powerful symbol than a flag. Flags are used by nation states to claim land and to announce their sovereign reign over the territory claimed by the placement of the flag. Loving a flag, what an odd object for love. Love is to be given to God and if we love God we love our fellow human beings. As a people we are to identify our allegiance with the reign of God, the people of God, the kingdom come.

Christianity is supposed to birth communities of 'called out ones' who meet in houses and serve one another until there is no poor among them. Buildings are to serve people not the aesthetics that denote wealth and power, or priests and the absurdity of celebrity pastors. Paul wrestled with celebrity in 1st. Cor. 1 as he challenged the schismatic persons who identified with a specific teacher as their ideal. These celebrity schismatic teachers aligned themselves with sacrificial persons (Paul, Peter, Apollos, and Jesus) while promoting themselves.

Humanity is one family and our faith is a border crossing faith where we come with peace, with feet that travel to build bridges of peace, love and understanding. Ethnicity vanishes when we walk in the Spirit. Our fellowship is with God and his children, not a denomination or a nation.

Teaching Christ Jesus is more than an altar call, it is an all-consuming life of living in a way that is inconsistent with the practices of the world. We are offensive to the world of power because we serve and do not lift up celebrities as models; we lift up exemplars and martyrs.

A Life Built on a Rock

Conviction

Who am I if I am not a child of God?
I have sought you with faith
Survived the pains of failure
Touched the sky and been blessed

You owned me when I was marred
A lost soul navigating a mad world
Your word was gentle and patient

I'm older now
My sail flies a little higher
The wind remains unpredictable
Perhaps its time to walk on water
One more time

I'm your servant, your slave
I've survived wind and sea
Your word is bold and driving

My conviction is buried deep in a lifetime
I know I have believed
I still believe
Through it all
I believe

All of these died in faith without having received the promises, but from a distance they saw and greeted them. They confessed that they were strangers and foreigners on the earth,

Heb 11:13

I Shall not be Moved

Life is a long journey and faith is chiseled into the soul by the wind and storms common to human beings. Faith is a wonderful part of human existence; it is for the spiritual person a tangible reality; as real as anything seen or touched.

Failure is a part of life, whether it be one's own weaknesses or the injustices of others and institutions that place one in the position of failure. A person needs a little self-determination and individuation to endure the pain of failure; both of these make one strong.

Most of us, at a very young age remember experiencing displeasure with the world we were born into. We soon become faced with ethical choices and our responses form our character in the midst of living. If we have faith, if we know God is watching, then we care deeply about how we choose to live.

Faith is always relational and not mere confession.

Soon decisions become responses born from an established character, a strong faith.

Over the course of life there are other grander moments of decision when faith and possibility bring God into the world, into our moment, into our life in such a way that we feel as though we are sailing the seas of chaos with Jesus in our boat. Once age and time set in our vigor fades, our activities change, yet many of us struggle with sitting still. Old and sure we enter the boat of faith and sail into the chaos knowing God is with us and whether we live or die is irrelevant to the one important thing; God is with us.

We have lived long enough, been through enough, that faith in all its power connects us with God and nothing can break faith's connection with the Spirit of life.

The Peace of Christ

False Religion

Peace of soul without peace in the world
You must close your eyes
Hide behind feeble religious lies
Live with an impotent faith
a god that hates justice

Religion that promotes violence
an abomination
Militarization of children
an abomination
the military is not faith's mission
souls of youth killed and killing
they are not the church's martyrs

Any religion that promotes violence
Idolatrous
Reading scripture without honesty
Immoral

The cost of wealth
intolerable in a world of poverty

Corporate abuse of humanity's world
A Murderous Crime

Christianity lost
to culturally determined values

Loving God with the mind
or
Lost to Dr. Feel Good

"Come to me, all you that are weary and are carrying heavy burdens, and I will give you rest. [29] Take my yoke upon you, and learn from me; for I am gentle and humble in heart, and you will find rest for your souls. [30] For my yoke is easy, and my burden is light."

Matt. 11:28

The Peace of Christ

God cares with the glory of his person about how he wins the heart and heals the world. God's peace lies in the rest of a divine confidence that once the revelation of God is understood, human beings willingly choose to follow God's ways and fall deeply in love with their heavenly father.

God seeks relationship not coerced submission.

As children of God, like our father, we bring healing and redemption into the world with a love as patient as time and empowered with life beyond the grave. Yet in the present age we live with an insatiable hunger in our being longing for a justice soaked in mercy and righteousness built up in faith.

The peace of Christ is the promise of a world where war is no longer taught and the imagination is captured with dreams of humanity liberated from her violence. Living with God's peace produces people with sane minds who seek change, risk their lives, and love living enough to value how they live if granted longevity and if not how is more important than another day.

A moral person images our moral God and brings their morality to scripture to form readings that change the world. Living ethically enables a person to consider others rather than fill their life with excess. As individuals the person of faith is immovable, as a member of humanity and the temple of Christ, they share with unmatched liberty.

The peace Jesus gives births people who refuse to deify institutions, listen to the Spirit, and walk with the voice of God. Those who do not know the peace of Christ hear the voice of Dr. Feel Good and seek their fulfillment in a culture of greed, like instinctual beasts.

Since there is a God

If there is a God

If there is a God
we would think god to be angry
If he were absent from the world
we would lose our humanity to violence
If God did not share his self with us
we would seek immortality by other means
If God did not relieve our suffering
we would blame him
If God does not to stop us on the path of self destruction
we will destroy ourselves

Searching for the origins of the universe
we accept the god of chance
Longing for meaning
we abandon morality and ethics for the vanity of beauty
In need of identity
we fail at the courage to be

Like angry gods we conquer creation,
we do so at the expense of our children
Fear drives the most powerful among us,
they rape humanity with war
We deify nation states
Our god is our tribe

God is not angry
God is patient
God longs to be present

We bring God into the world when we reject violence
Immortality cannot be attained
Life is God's gift to his children
Faith in God provides meaning,
when meaning is undone by human cruelty

Without Faith in God
we are lost on a path of madness
To be loved of God is enough to birth courage to be
Creation is healed as humanity lives morally
draws near to God
We are to be one
Nationalism is tribalism
In Christ all humanity can rest

To conquer one's self is the call of God
Fear is lost
faith abides forever
We will learn war no more
Salvation has come
Our savior has shown us how to live

I, the Teacher, when king over Israel in Jerusalem, ¹³ applied my mind to seek and to search out by wisdom all that is done under heaven; it is an unhappy business that God has given to human beings to be busy with.

Ecc 1:12-13

Yes, there is a God

I think the portrayals of God as angry in scripture are more a reflection of humanity than of God. I think when God acts in the world that God acts from the divine love. We seem to lack insight into the metaphysical reality of the collective spirit of humanity and **I don't believe in an angry God.** its connection to the physical world. We undo creation, we resist goodness, God stays away, keeps distance, his elusive presence leaves us feeling alone.

Often God is portrayed as violent in scripture. The violent depictions of God in the Old Testament are more a reflection of human failure to hear, of the entrenched violence in our perceptions of reality. How God's voice is discerned in the OT is often through human experience and thought. The OT is a history of a people and their failure (our failure) to discern God without error. However God is not violent, rather violence is indigenous to humanity and we release violence into the world like a magnetic pulse. Creation convulses under the evil brought into the world by human beings. Understanding that God is not the creation allows us to separate the metaphysical upheaval from God, yet God is responsible for creation so we see God in the upheaval.

Our ability to conceive of a life without death is indicative of the image of God that we bear. We seek immortality as though it were our birthright, yet like God it eludes us and the enemy 'death' holds sway over our lives. It is religious belief, faith alone that can provide human beings with a reason to hope for more than this life. Our creator longs for our redemption and is patient as we move toward the ultimate embrace of eternal life.

It is God, it is faith, that brings relief to us in the midst of our suffering. Without this power we would blame God and never grasp the love of God in redemption. In the words of Paul the suffering of this present age can in no wise compare with the weight of glory to be revealed in us.

Will visions of apocalypse come to pass or can humanity correct their erring way and surrender to the non-violent God?

The denial of God as relevant in an age of science professing to have uncovered the origins of the universe is to exalt the creature above the creator. The imaginative power of the human mind to even attempt to have any credibility in regards to the origin of the universe is indicative of the image of God in humanity. However grand our science, we fall short of exemplifying intelligent life because of our self-destructive practices through war and the greed that consumes the resources of the world by a few.

The beauty of a cathedral is always indicative of human suffering. Somebody suffered so the love for art and architecture could outshine the picture of real life where the poor suffer. The practice of art and building should never be at the cost of human life.

The hostility of the earth, the inevitability of death drive an unspoken justification for abuse and oppression for the sake of alleged progress. Under this same sense of justification is practiced an unregulated consumption of creation's resources. The voice of God in death is enough to provoke resentment towards the belief in a completely good God; sacrificial progress becomes historical achievement and begins the deification of the rulers of the earth.

The vanity of it all, the ever-learning never changing human being remains as ethically immoral as their primitive ancestors who built the first cities. Human progress without inner change, without moral conscience, without ethical development only leads to technological distancing from the barbarism of the past. We now kill people more efficiently, we destroy the earth with radiation for unknown periods of time.

We study the cosmos, the molecular structures of the physical world, yet we fail to face our fear of mortality, our endless cycles of violence, our metaphysical connectedness as humanity with both creation and one another. So, *Jesus' vision of God enabled him to live a wholly human life.* we miss the voice of wisdom, the voice of God, calling us patiently to face our failures, our rebellion, our ignorance of faith.

Jesus Refuses to be Alone

Resurrection

An indomitable hope
Resting in a living image
a consciousness of god likeness
a sacredness given
it cannot be murdered
life will rise from the ground

Resurrection is God's love
A tangible reality whose taste is like a smile
The miracle of a person
Humanity is the apex of creation
The treasure of God
Hidden in the cosmos
Awaiting a day of revealing

The unimaginable became inevitable
The omnific one
entered the adventure
became the creature
Humanity made immortal
embraced into the eternal one

Spirit hovers over human reality
The unseen over the unseen
a voice cries up from the earth
death murder
suffering injustice
greed violence
Can the almighty finish his beginning?

The victory of God contained in a vessel of clay
an unprecedented unrepeatable event
God clothed once forever a person
a lowly life
a treasure hidden
a victim of evil
God revealed
a life
never to be lost
a Spirit alive beyond death
reborn embodied humanity

Jesus refuses to be alone
we will join him

[10] that I may know him and the power of his
resurrection, and may share his sufferings,
becoming like him in his death,

Phil 3:10

Never Lost

The God who created and lifted us up from the ground, from the
dust, can cause us to rise up once we have returned to the earth like
ashes. The heavens declare the glory of God and only humanity
can appreciate the view of such a spectacular display of power, of
order and disorder, of a vastness meant to communicate God as
an external testimony, a testimony matched only by the internal
testimony of God in the moral conscience.

God the source of life, the giver of life, has placed resurrection in the soul of humanity and laughed at death in the joy of Jesus' endurance. Resurrection is sewn into the fabric of reality; it is as tangible as faith for those who know God. Abel will rise to melt away the pain of Cain in the presence of God and smile with all of history's murdered souls.

Within the glory of the cosmos God has placed the treasure of his longing, we are the desire of God. The creation of humanity was an event without precedent never to be repeated. The mystery of human consciousness, moral judgment, disjunctive relationship to the natural world, and wonder at the reason for mortality all witness to the work of God. God is creating a family to share in the work of creation, the canvas of God's power and artistry. The joy was so intensely overwhelming that God joined the creation through humanity and made being human a part of God's self.

The beginning of God's work is marked with the freedom of humanity so that we might choose, grow to know, be consumed with one reality; our complete and absolute dependency upon God. Learning to hate injustice, learning to become agents of redemption bringing God into the world as living temples up from the ground, we reveal the light that pierces darkness.

Jesus the firstborn of humanity calls us to follow on a path that leads to embrace into the being of God.

Like Adam, Jesus will not be alone.

Mercy and Madness

They shall know I Am

Rivers of blood mark history
It is the way of little gods
filling the world with death
God mocks the power of a demagogue

The Nile ran with blood
God's message of mercy
Down by the river
On their knees they dug for the water of life
Oppressors in the position of slaves

Instruction failed
Mercy mistaken for weakness
A fleshly heart
Turns to stone

War is ruthless
Unrestrained destruction wins

The creator of life
of water and blood
is refused

Plagues and Mercy follow
The contest turns
Kill Moses - kill them all

Such love for Egypt
They shall know that I am Yahweh
A tragic moment in the life of God

Remember
The cost of Israel's deliverance
God captured in a mess

Death comes without murder
The firstborn die
God weeps
An event never to be repeated

A momentary release – time to run
Faithless power rises again
Kill them all

War is madness worshiping at the carcass of a slain dragon
Peace is possible
Let my people go

Jesus wept
God and humanity reconciled on a cross

I will harden Pharaoh's heart, and he will pursue them, so that I
will gain glory for myself over Pharaoh and all his army; and the
Egyptians shall know that I am the LORD. And they did so.

Exod 14:4

They Shall Know that I Am Yahweh

"They shall know that I am Yahweh" is called 'the recognition formula' by academics. It is a steady refrain in scripture. God is concerned about his 'self revelation' accomplished through his relationship with Israel. God thinks about both Israel and the people with whom God interacts while nurturing Israel. God is also con-

> *We cannot simply learn about God, we must learn about ourselves in relation to God.*

cerned about how humanity is revealed in the interaction of God's redemptive history. He is concerned that we learn about ourselves.

The deliverance of Israel from Egypt is marked with moments that reveal God's care for Egypt. Of course God could have defeated Egypt in a moment, rather God was patient with Egypt, with Pharaoh, and the plagues counter Egypt's worship of cosmological deities with signs that indicate Yahweh (alone) is Lord over all creation. Each plague is seasoned with mercy so that Egypt will not be destroyed. God was not giving Egypt to the Israelites, he was preserving Egypt so that they might know that he is 'the LORD'.

The initial plague is a sign of how king's war; they fill the world with blood. The blood red Nile signals two realities. God controls the arterial bloodline to the heart of Egypt; their water supply. God is also Lord of all life and creator of the blood that flows through the human body. In this single act God could have defeated the Egyptians by cutting off their water supply, but God was merciful and they found fresh water by digging in the sand along the banks. This act of mercy makes God a poor war strategist and Pharaoh views this act of mercy as weakness.

The death of the firstborn of Egypt is an act that God is forced into. Pharaoh has sworn to kill Moses and so a slaughter of Israelites would ensue for Pharaoh plans to release his dogs of war. God has been both patient and merciful throughout the plague narratives. Now God must stop Pharaoh, it is a disturbing act of power and loss of life.

It is the great cost that God pays for Israel, God's self revelation, how God is perceived, is all touched by this moment; a moment never to be repeated.

Yes, God loves all humanity including those in power, those guilty of living in luxury at the expense of others. Yet God wants the oppressed liberated and the powerful to learn mercy and justice. The Passover is about many theological truths, this one is overlooked, God was displeased with the outcome of his battle with Pharaoh.

> God is not at war with humanity, his surrender of love is Jesus' lesson from a cross.

The battle with Pharaoh ultimately ends in the lesson that war is madness. Madness alone accounts for the pursuit of the slaves into the sea after the lived drama of the plagues and the deaths of the firstborn.

God's revelation continues and is fulfilled in the death of God on a cross. The murder of God takes place everyday human beings persist with injustice and harden their hearts to the plight of the poor and oppressed.

Heart and Reason

Immoral Reading

Violence reigns, morality fails
The crashing wave of religious authority stymies the imagination
Presses against the past
Defies the dead
Rejects the visiting of iniquity

Judge for yourself
Walk the path of the lonely
It is one person wide
Few resolute souls press forward

God said
Did he?
It is written but not understood
I cannot abandon goodness
Bury the dead
Read again

Shall not God do right?
God speaks in the heart
Through stories littered with human error

Science progresses
Humanity has not
Nor has Christian faith

Now is the time
Dead bones must live

A people of peace will prevail
Christianity must die in order to live

Scripture remains
Revealing God
Exposing humanity
Abusers of God
of one another

Faith is not impotent
Hope rests in the people of God
Progress is obedience
Progress is reading scripture as a moral being

[14] When Gentiles, who do not possess the law, do instinctively what the law requires, these, though not having the law, are a law to themselves. [15] They show that what the law requires is written on their hearts, to which their own conscience also bears witness;

Rom 2:14-15

Escaping the Errors of the Past

God is the moral being. Because human beings are created in the image of God, they possess a moral conscience. Faith and the pursuit of God through loving (a good) God and loving humanity enhance the moral conscience to live with a vision consistent with God's will. Scriptural reading guided by a person with an enhanced moral conscience is superior to scriptural reading guided by reason alone. A moral conscience guided by love for all humanity is superior to the ethically argued compromises of institutional powers, both church and state.

The failure of the church impacts the world. When the church lives out Christ, the world is blessed. She has failed for too long and too often. Immoral readings of scripture do not discern the commandeering of the voice of God by the state, or the use of oracular formulas by less than exemplary people. These immoral readings replace the Spirit with teachings that are incompatible with the reign of God.

If scripture is read correctly then all the powers of Biblical interpretation are guided by a person whose vision of God is consistent with Jesus' and whose moral conscience questions those passages that lack the mercy that identifies our redeeming Father.

The god depicted in popular evangelical circles, in the ignorance of PSA Theory is not a god that I like. God is more than, always more than our thoughts. God is love, not a judicial tyrant.

Innocence Lost

Inside of Me

Somewhere inside of me
There is the taste of everything being alright
How is this possible?
This tormenting hope of joy,
never fulfilled
At moments its scent fills the air
It touches reality

I dream of those moments extending into time
I find God there
I don't want him to go away

Was it I who failed?
But I am not alone
People all around
The walls go up
The healer leaves

Aw to be unclothed
Shame shutters, fearing being un-forgiven
Vulnerability needs comfort from the Holy one
There is no space for condemnation
When God is near

What have I done?
This is the cry of error
You were born a victim of sin
We hurt one another just by being

Jesus' demanded his own baptism
a baptism of repentance
a mature soul knows their innocence lost

Shall we shame the other
Or only ourselves
Is forgiveness real?
Does love heal?

We can be changed
no longer the same
Can we be new together?
Acceptance
Equality
One day the race will be over.

He drove out the man; and at the east of the garden of Eden he placed the cherubim, and a sword flaming and turning to guard the way to the tree of life.

Gen 3:24

The Human Condition

We are individuals yet we are not. We were created to be relational and not to be alone. We inherit a world where the remnants of those who came before us form the familial, social, political and religious constructs that impart to us habits of behavior and educational formation. We begin with a sweet innocence and lose it so easily. Reality visits us with the lawlessness of our ancestors; it is the way God made the world.

Belief in God is easy when life is still fresh as a gift and wonder fills all we see. How quickly we are evicted from the garden! To return we must pass a flaming sword, as word it cuts to the marrow of our soul, as a weapon it murders others. Yet that innocence calls within for a world of existence free from this horrid inheritance of a history of sins. If only this train we ride wasn't real, if only we could simply disembark into a new world.

We live with the shame of sins unknown, sins forgotten, sin with repercussions that seem endless. Our failure to love, to forgive, to hope, to live in Eden while in the land of wandering disables the spiritually harmonious life God desires for us. Nothing touches reality like mortality. Death is the voice of God saying we are not fit to live as we are. Death is God's severest judgment; death is God's enemy. Death also provides excuse for living life in a selfish way, in a 'sinful' way.

Mortality is a great test, it develops an ethical soul, it calls forth love, it demands repentance, it requires suffering for love to prevail, it eliminates self-importance; it opens the soul to ultimate dependency upon God.

God forgives us. We must forgive God for the pains of Death.

What have I done if I have not learned to forgive, to love, to receive the healing that comes from God and allows entrance into a new creation, a return to a garden where innocence and maturity meld into life everlasting?

Jeremiah and Paul's Lament

Minstrel or Mystic

Perhaps I should have been a minstrel
It has been a long road
From a small child I have these memories
They remain like a burning bush
never consumed ever present

Divine moments of revelation
Formative power directing my soul
A call from somewhere unlike here
Even in failure the memories hold me

They tell me who I am
Even when I am not
Linked to life like an eternal thread
Piercing beyond the present

Bound to the temporal
These memories
Without them I cease

These days they mix with pain.
misunderstandings, aging, illness,
and an insatiable longing for more

Blinded by light that I might see
I am not like you, you are not me
The richness of God has touched me
No one cares but I

When I read scripture
My consciousness is invaded with thoughts
Some never to be shared
We are so slow to receive God into the world

This vessel of clay, this broken soul,
both have served as a temple for God
I am humbled
Alone in a world of people

But, as it is written,
"What no eye has seen, nor ear heard,
nor the human heart conceived,
what God has prepared for those who love him"

First Cor. 2:9

Calling and Isolation

Jeremiah and Paul were persons set aside at birth to be formed by events in their life so that they might be used by God. Each of them experienced uniqueness as vessels set aside for speaking truth to their generation and into the ages. Paul was more independent and obstinate than Jeremiah, yet a careful reading of his letters reveals moments of painful exclusion and loneliness.

Both Jeremiah and Paul were educated, both understood their life experiences to be formative for their calling. Each of these men experienced revelation that defied the religious conventions of their time. They were both subjected to incarceration, torture, and attempts to take their lives. However, they both lived to become old men.

It seems that each were overcome with an invasion of their consciousness, an invasion that carried their thoughts to places not yet imagined. Jeremiah releases some of his revelation in the 'new covenant' (Jeremiah 31:31-34). Paul's revelation was a mystical experience which left him wondering whether or not he had left his body (died) and opened his mind to thoughts that humanity was yet unprepared for, or unable to hear (2nd Cor. 12).

I think that, the practice of imagining the transformation of the world is a theological and spiritual exercise. It is not simply the imagining of how the world is supposed to be, but the imagining of how we are to submit ourselves to God on the path that takes us there. That is imagining how to demonstrate the world to come in the present. In Christianity, this is a communal exercise and yet requires the presence of that word taught by those who have been called. Although the canon of scripture is closed, the living word, embodied in suffering servants, captured in writings, adds life to the body of Christ.

Religious interpreters can close the canon but they cannot silence the truth shared in the heart of lives that communicate more than their systems, they cannot silence the writings of those that read with greater clarity and share new thoughts of the kingdom come.

The Tower of Futility

When History Collides

Unspoken powers visited upon us
A world in crisis with only the present in sight
Always running from the past
Unable to face the truth
All are children of their fathers

Unable to steer a different course
nothing new under the sun
myths of human progress exposed
no change
Everything remains the same

Sins of the past piling up in the present
Generations captured in a spiral
Humanity created to be one

Prophets, Poets, and Troubadours
all seem to know
Its the same ole road we've taken before

Rushing madly towards collapse
War cries abound
Christianity absorbed by national identity
Now ruin lies ahead

Greed and Empire
must be restrained
cost of her consumption
cannot be sustained

Violence cannot end
When history collides
Will we ever learn?

and said, "Thus far shall you come, and no farther,
and here shall your proud waves be stopped?"

Job 38:11

They All Fall Down

The unbounded arrogance of human government to produce weapons capable of destroying the earth that God created is the ultimate hubris. It is imperative that the people of God pray that the fall of a technologically advanced society does not take the world with it.

The domination of humanity by the ascendency of state powers continually expanding their self-interest at the expense of others is a doomed enterprise. This effort is always nationalist, militaristic and materialistic. In the economy of God we are meant to serve one another. In the economy of empire, humanity is not equal, and the resources of the earth are hoarded for the few.

This cyclic reality of a few demagogues who perennially pursue immortality through historical memory *Death is the great equalizer of humanity.* is an absurdity. Jesus taught that the greatest among us is a servant. Jesus' concept of a servant is not compatible with cultural claims like 'military service' or 'civil servant'.

Preserving the right of people to live unmolested by other nations requires respecting the truth that the earth and all the many peoples that populate the world belong to God. In the faith and theology of scripture Eve is the mother of all living; we are one family.

From time to time, history collides upon its self. It is as though some unstoppable force takes humanity down a path towards self-destruction; unless saner souls are willing to restructure and let go of national pride and domination of others. God has made the world and created humanity to be divided off into cultural-linguistic independent groups of people. This one fact creates the dynamic that ultimately halts the hegemony of empire.

The reign of God is not consistent with the governmental systems of human history. The reign of God is an in-breaking power insisting upon peace established through justice and righteousness. The justice of God is not the penal concept of justice; it is the right of every human being to food, clothing, shelter, education, and health care. The righteousness of God is not the petty sin identifying works of ineffective religion; it is to live in conjunction with wisdom (creation) and in loving, sharing relationship with others.

The People of God

Hope for a Better World

God's hope for humanity
A People
God's desire for a dwelling place
A People
Hope for a better world
A People

To be called
To speak truth to power
To possess moral force
The righteousness of Spirit
These are superior to temporal structures

Love's objects
God and Humanity
no other commands

Change comes
not by celebrity,
not through mass conversion,
not in institutions
Change comes by works of love
In a people

A people in exile
Don't get too comfortable
A people of love
Give it all

Sell the cathedral
Educate the poor
Sell the satellite broadcast
Plant seeds that grow food
Language learning is to truly speak in tongues

Teach peace to your children
Hating weapons of war is righteousness
Hating corporate greed is righteousness
Hating racism is righteousness

Be merciful to the orphan
Pursuit of a dream is better than longevity

But this is the covenant that I will make with the house of Israel after those days, says the LORD: I will put my law within them, and I will write it on their hearts; and I will be their God, and they shall be my people.

Jer 31:33

A People who Serve

To be the people of God is to be those who show the world God through our manner of living, through our ethical choices, through a relentless willingness to remake the world in accordance with the reign of God. As the people of God, those in Christ Jesus, we share a universal cultural ethos regardless of the nation state in which we live or of the language we speak or of the social status we attain by virtue of wealth or education. The Christian people's first and sole allegiance is to God; this means God's concern for the welfare of others is our concern.

If we focused more on being a people and less on the feeble attempts at permanence through institutional structures, if we chose humility over pride, if we thought of others rather than the size and architecture of a building, if we rejected the endless accumulation of power and shared with the least among us; then we could be a people.

With eighty percent of the world's population living on ten dollars a day the monies provided to those who claim to do ministry must be spent in a way that loves humanity, this demonstrates love for God. God is not interested in the size or grandeur of church buildings, nor is God interested in the celebrity minister, God desires a people who shun celebrity and recognize the labor of those who risk their life, resist the powers of injustice, and live out the scripture.

Economic decisions are unethical if God's love and care for the poor are not the guiding concern.

The era of stadium crusades is over; the era of belief in the power of broadcasting is over, and the era of the mega church will come to an end. Organized communities that educate and reach out to the poor is the direction the church was always intended to take. The world changes, but Christian practice remains the same; unfortunately the errors are always built on injustice, on compromise with the state rather than toleration and resistance.

We can educate a generation to reject violence and live out a life consistent with the reign and Spirit of God. We will also need to model for them the path that leads to the way of Jesus.

Faith a Tangible Reality

Only Believing

Belief alone explains being human
Consciousness needs a body,
needs an other
Faith becomes a tangible reality,
a part of creation

A creature of an incompatible origin
Disjunctive in relation to nature
A dreaming spirit embodied to live
Imaging a grandeur beginning

Finding God in the unseen
The unseen reality of thought
A sense of divinity within
An incomprehensible lack

I believe in believing
The fact of faith
There is one God
Our Father

I believe in revelation
God revealed in flesh
Jesus makes sense of reality
Faith's tangible Son

yet for us there is one God, the Father, from whom are all things and for whom we exist, and one Lord, Jesus Christ, through whom are all things and through whom we exist.

First Cor. 8:6

More than Dirt

Children know we are more than flesh, more than all other creatures. Children feel the freshness of life as incomprehensible gift. Children remind us we were born to believe. Their innocence connects us, and reminds us, of our own beginnings. For a short time the sins of the world are foreign to them, like an intrusion into higher expectations. It is this primal innocence that we hear when a human being, after committing some horrendous act, declares 'it wasn't me'. We soon pass from innocent victims to complicit perpetrators unless we are reared correctly, taught to believe, and our innocence protected.

Believing in goodness is like a primal instinct that must be nurtured if we are to grow in faith. The object of our belief is the work of God; it is God's self revelation found externally present in nature and internally present in the story of scripture. *We were created to be good, to be Christians.* Believing is an act of resistance against the chaos of creation; it is furthered in response to scripture's story of God. Believing makes life possible; it inhibits the desire of flesh to preserve itself at any cost.

In 1st Corinthians 8:6 Paul the apostle opens the Shema (Deuteronomy 6:4) to embrace the seen and the unseen, the father and the son, the word become flesh. This work of God to join humanity reveals the goodness of God as self-giving love. The incomprehensible, the invisible, the unseen has become communicable through a human life, a story connected to the work of God in humanity. We need only believe.

The gospel is the story that resonates with our soul, speaks to the moral conscience, and brings awareness of the image of God in us.

Interviewing Wisdom

Counseling with Qohelet

Hey old man can you tell me a story?
Can you make sense of your life?
It's so hard when it's live
A whirlwind of love and disaster

How have you survived?
Are your stories real or a lie?
The pain of dislike, rejection
I was a victim before I even tried

Is there meaning in the world?
What is the pain I see in your eyes?
Love defies meaning
Hope endures pain

Is your smile a lie or a sign of madness?
I've reached my limits
nothing left but to cry

Can you make everything alright?
You can't undo the past
There is only the moment

Is there nothing that lasts?
The search for meaning endures

Is power always oppressive?
Human beings were not meant to hold power over one another

What is the most threatening evil?
Desire over thankfulness.

Which is greater power or wisdom?
Wisdom is divine but power kills the divine.

Where is wisdom found?
In powerlessness

How shall I live?
Seek wisdom, avoid power,
Die in peace, all else is vanity.

There is an evil that I have seen under the sun, and it lies heavy upon humankind: those to whom God gives wealth, possessions, and honor, so that they lack nothing of all that they desire, yet God does not enable them to enjoy these things, but a stranger enjoys them.

Ecc 6:1-2

Before Derrida there was Qohelet

Qohelet is the author of the book known by its Latin title as Ecclesiastes. Qohelet's story is the reflections of a child of wealth who witnesses the effects of power upon his father. The power his father does not possess is the power to find wisdom.

Stories help us make sense of the world in the face of meaninglessness. The story of Qohelet, the king of wisdom, is a story of a privileged son whose father lost his money, his mind and his son in pursuit of more. The wisdom of Qohelet was impossible without the experience that formed his life. An educated mind captured in a life of obscurity, separated from the goodness of life by a grievous evil; the uncontrolled desire for more in his father, a desire that led to destitution for his son and lifelong depression for his self.

From the harsh vantage of reality, Qohelet became a deconstructionist who refused the traditions of his age. He claimed that Kings (even Solomon) are not wise, they are possessed with uncontrolled desire and endless vanity. He saw life was absurd in relation to wisdom; the princes of wisdom were slaves to the fools of power. Qohelet learned that wisdom exists in the ethical life of the poor who see the world as a lie.

> *Only the poor know the truth about power in the world. Wisdom is their gift.*

More than a Feeling

Heart Speech

From the pulsating power of the heart
flows the thought that forms speech
Love is always an intellectual exercise
Love is more than feeling

Heart speech appears irrational
Yet cuts to the depth of existence
Heart speech is theological
Birthed in the furnace of faith
Where the absurd meets meaning

Words void of truth
Pleasant to the ear
Reveal a deceptive heart
The smiling clown of illusion

An open heart is an honest discourse
A refusal to settle for less than the will of God
Obstinate conviction ready to die without a fight
Truth ground to dust will rise
To be spoken in the mouth of the spiritually intelligent lover

Love is a teacher
Love abhors ignorance
Love's words liberate the world

The good person out of the good treasure of the heart produces good, and the evil person out of evil treasure produces evil; for it is out of the abundance of the heart that the mouth speaks.

Luke 6:45

Loving God is an Intellectual Exercise

Love is a relational negotiation and is subject to moments of irrational action. Love can appear to be irrational because love is eternal; however love subverts reality with the mind of God. Love is self-sacrificial like a teacher nurturing the immature, the ignorant, the wicked. Love is creative speech that shakes leviathan by the tail and dances upon the backs of crocodiles.

Love speaks, there is no disconnect between the heart and the mind, between the speech and the act. To love is to learn, to face reality, to embrace wisdom with erotic passion and unshakeable faithfulness. God does not produce foolish children. God redeems our foolishness with insight that communicates the way of God into our world, our culture, our society.

Claiming to love and refusing to learn is to go about crippled, blind, and imprisoned. We are called to love God with our minds. A theology of love is not mere empathy or prayer from an ivory tower, it is the audacity to speak truth whether acceptance or rejection follows.

Jesus refuses to separate love from speech, or speech from action.

A Little Wickedness

Pressed

A little rebellion is good for the soul
Refusing claims perceived to be God's
Questioning cleanses the soul

God has big shoulders
Honesty is preferable to unquestioned submission
Scripture stimulates
Morality touches
Intellect wrestles
Spirit answers

The ever-present kiss of mortality is God's love
Speaking, calling, drawing the reality of faith
out of unimaginable suffering
Life is sweet like sunlight
and
often presses down upon us with the weight of hell

Despair, the friend of poets and death
Out of the press rises beauty
Within the press is the descent to nothingness

The poet knows
asceticism leads to madness
wisdom needs restrained
life is lived in the midst of pain

A little wine can gladden the heart
A little blues can keep ya sane
Joy is always a new day

[16] Do not be too righteous, and do not act too wise; why should you destroy yourself? [17] Do not be too wicked, and do not be a fool; why should you die before your time?

Ecc 7:16-17

God's Shoulders

Our father's shoulders are strong enough to carry our weakness, our failures, and our discomfort, big enough to challenge the perceptions of God passed on to us through the power of religious indoctrination. We are all learning to live and we all face the struggles of life in a world not the way it is supposed to be. The gospel is good news, God loves the life he has created and is with us in our suffering. God is that whisper of will that lifts us out of the press of despair and turns pain into hope for a better day, a better world.

Every good answer needs a better question. Every question needs new thoughts, fresh words, and a little color that turns ashes into beauty. Christianity cannot be reduced to humanism, but humanism is closer to Jesus than religious nonsense. We should bring a party everyday to the sick, the lame, the dying, the poor, the oppressed, the prisoners and the addicted. Instead religious people hide behind walls and speak about transcendence. They make sinners out of the righteous who share their food in desperation. Only a fool smiles all the time, or a clown, or a hypocrite, there is no best life on this side of the grave.

It is better to stand at a distance from those who think themselves to be righteous, and then, with your hand on your chest, ask

God for mercy. Holiness is God's nature, not a code. Holiness is to draw near to God in faith with sincere honesty and seek to be a lover of God and humanity. There is no authority except that which comes from God and all other temporal powers are not God.

Share your sorrows, give to the poor, grow some food, build someone a house, sing a song that allows for healing tears to flow, leave the mega church and become a follower of Jesus; do justice, love mercy, walk humbly with God.

Love is Holiness

Love is a Promise

Love doesn't come without promise
Destiny is a myth
A soul mate is only as good as their promise

To make a promise is a divine act
To live out a promise is to be divine
Love is not an ethereal mist
mere emotion
a potion for the alchemist and the gypsy

God is love
Love is not God
God defines love with promises
Promises fulfilled
Promises to come
Promises upheld by the nature of God

To love another human being like God
is to embrace all the pain of holding onto another
Love overcomes frailty of mind and body
Love is a weapon against the darkness of death

Love is a surrender of self
Love never lets go
Love never fails because God is love
In the end God wins

God is the irresistible lover of the ages
the flesh embracing creator of humanity
A father to prodigals
The lover of the world

That at the name of Jesus every knee should bow, of things in heaven, and things in earth, and things under the earth; And that every tongue should confess that Jesus Christ is Lord, to the glory of God the Father.

Phil 2:10-11

Love Wins

It is a grievous mistake to think that the confession of every tongue is in any way, with any tongue, an act of coercion accomplished through any real or perceived threat from God. Rather it is the knowledge and grace contained in understanding the unfolding revelation of God's self in time that wins the hearts (tongues) and the bowed knee of all creation. God is not in a hurry in this effort to win over all as God communicates God's nature, holiness, God's self to the record of history and the soul of every human being.

Hell is our own creation; it is to be abolished, lost to a consuming fire. God is not willing that any perish. The mercy of God is not constrained to the religious claims of those who read scripture like a rulebook. There are unknowns in scripture, questions unanswered, not even asked. The Bible is the most misused book in any and every church and by every group of power decreeing institutional finality on meaning.

Keep your promises, love deeper, cry more, be faithful to those God has laid at the gate of your life, you will find God suffering at the threshold of doors closed to hospitality for the poor, the oppressed, the trafficked, the souls who never see goodness from humanity.

God has no concern for relics, empty cathedrals rich with art, pilgrimages to alleged holy places. God loves the neighbor that is ignored by the power of organized religion. The greatest among us is always the suffering servant of all, the servant whose pilgrimage is marked by contact with those that too many of us ignore.

In Honor of an Exemplary People

Muddy Mississippi

Baptized in the muddy Mississippi
Learned to sing in a gospel choir
Touched by God
Loved my screaming preacher

Met Jesus as a small child
Didn't need the waters of the Jordan
My deliverance was from a rope
My salvation a song of freedom
Our Joshua an abolitionist of immovable moral force
Our Esther ran a railroad
Our prophet educated at Morehouse

My promise land a dream
My pilgrimage an inward journey
a mountain from where justice rolls

I crossed a bridge in Alabama
Jesus walked with me
righteousness was a march
My people have always been exiles

The blues my spiritual discipline
Prayer burst forth without a manual
Mama knew Jesus
taught me to love my way through the mess

Mama's wailing wall was a fortress of racism
Papa's battle was for dignity as a man
Our faith saved the faith
That we believed against the tide of lies,
a miracle, a testimony to the power of truth

Our holy land
the ground on which we were planted
A people of God
A grand history

And when we cried unto the LORD God of our fathers, the LORD heard our voice, and looked on our affliction, and our labor, and our oppression:

Deut 26:7

Un-borrowed History

One of the great wonders of American history is the acceptance of Christian faith by a people held as slaves, subjected to racism, and abused with religious fervor. This fact attests to the power of the scriptures even when they are used to justify evil. African Americans produced one of the greatest religious traditions in U.S. history. The 'black' church produced Pentecostalism, the ring shout, call and response, gospel music and spirituality upheld by community. The most amazing people in American history are African Americans who excelled in the face of oppressive socio-political powers.

The gospel is always about the liberation of the poor and oppressed. The dignity required to rise above an assigned station in life and overcome the majority is representative of a power dependent upon an uncompromising faith in goodness, not the goodness of man, but of God. The image of God in human beings holding to faith is irrepressible. God can be found in the life stories of African Americans whose lives and stories continue to inspire the generations.

The African Americans; Fredrick Douglass, Harriet Tubman, Mary Mcleod Bethune, W.E.B. DuBois, Martin Luther King Jr. are only a few heroes of American history and Christian faith. The collected folk tales of 'Uncle Remus' resident in the African American people display a subversive awareness reflective of Jesus' stories in the gospels.

It is unfortunate that the dominant story of the faith of the western European American is more like the book of Joshua than the gospels.

Little Human Beings

I am a Child

I speak
I think
I listen
I'm a child

You can lie if you like
I see the world with my own eyes
Why do you think I cry?

I feel just like you
But my tears are not always the same
I'm adjusting to the pain of living

I know I have so much to learn
I'm sorry you're so afraid, so worried
I like to hear you sing

My grandma is bent, weak, she sleeps a lot
My grandpa is slow but refuses to stop
I see my end in them

You can't hide it from me
The world is cruel
I know there are monsters
I would rather die than be one

I feel him sometimes; God
Mostly when you hold me

Or when I have a good dream
Or when my grandpa tells me God touches him
I want to be a good person
Will you teach me how?

"It is easier to build strong children than to repair broken men."

—Fredrick Douglas

The wolf shall live with the lamb, the leopard
shall lie down with the kid,
the calf and the lion and the fatling together,
and a little child shall lead them.

Isa 11:6

Innocence and Intellect

Children are amazing compilations of hope, resilience and life. Like every generation they hope to be better than their forefathers. Their capacity to recover from hurt feelings is lost too soon to the lingering memory of resentment and time. Their lives each testify to the immortality of humanity, a fleeting hope, and a living possibility in the goodness of faith.

These little ones learn so quickly to speak, think and listen that their very existence testifies to the miracle of creation, of humanity as the apex of God's work. They discover the truth of reality and hide from it with imagination. It is the call of adults to nurture their imagination with thoughts that heal the present, with a hope capable of enduring all that would withstand its vision and most importantly with a life rooted in stories of faith.

With the ease of a well-trained psychologist, children know how to comfort their own parents in moments when words are replaced with touch. At the same moment their own need for a little selfishness, their own dependency draws them into the grasp of love. They learn that love is both need and relationship, that love heals the pain of reality. At this point these responses are instinctually existential and not yet articulate comprehension. Their minds like spirit are awake and ready to be taught. Their innocence leans into the threshold of an inescapable mess; of a world needing God to be fully present.

They need a history, a story, and an example of how one love's their way through a world of brokenness. They need honesty; they need the loving connection of a child with the wisdom of the aged. It is the meeting of beginning and ending that holds the promise of faith's knowing that the story holds eternity in its grasp; that God who creates, never loses his children.

The Table of the Lord

A World Transformed

The banquet of God
A seat for every soul
Need met in mutual sharing
Everyone invited

The beggar, the insane,
the crippled, the lame
the loose woman
the degenerate man

His teaching in flesh
His blood shed in violence
The wonder of eternity
God on a cross

Nourish yourself on the flesh of Christ
Drink the blood that absorbed all violence
Acknowledge the silencing of God
an event overcome by resurrection

Imagine a world without money
Where human worth prohibits greed
This is the sacred calling of God's people
A Eucharistic celebration of humanity
embraced into the living Christ

The table of the Lord is not a crumb and a sip
It is a world transformed by a people
who insist on 'no poor among them'

Do this
live out the teaching of Jesus
Do this
remember the gift of God

He defied reality
He was unrealistic
He believed in the deification of humanity
Peacemaking children of God

From his shoulders he cast a mountain of weight into the sea
and brought to life a new humanity
aliens, exiles, visionaries, dreamers
a people who refuse the world as it is

The table of the Lord is not a piece of furniture
It is a feast of peace
Where the oppressed are set free
Where the will of the Lord is done
Where debt is released
Where the name of God is hallowed
Not by a ceremony
But by a people

For all who eat and drink without discerning the body, eat and drink judgment against themselves.

First Cor 11:29

The Preservation of Content

Ceremonial form is symbolic of a greater meaning. The purpose of ceremonial form is to produce meaning and meaning cannot be articulated in words alone but must enter the world as practice. The goal of memory is to enrich an on going story that is consistent with the original event(s) that inspired the ceremony; not as an end but as a tool. When the ceremonial fails to produce an ongoing story consistent with the original event(s) and fails to remain true to the meaning of those events, we receive a form separated from the original reality. In the case of the Eucharist it is the absence of a love feast where the rich serve the poor in tangible ways that fulfill the social vision of Jesus that manifests the reign of God in the world.

The sacralizing of a ceremony results in an institutional power that limits the original impact of the event(s) that birthed the need for a practice that keeps the meaning of those events in the forefront of the masses. It is not the ceremony nor the sip and the crumb that are sacred, it is the people who are humanized and experience the reign of God by living out the meaning in the present.

I do not think a robed caste of priests claiming infallibility was the intent of Jesus when he was washing Peter's feet. Jesus connected his life and death to the one practice that defined his ministry as sinful; he ate with the unclean, he was called a glutton and a wino. The marginalized, the outsiders, the unclean, did not make Jesus unclean, rather his acceptance, his teaching, his love and his insistence on love of the one left on the side of the road defined his table fellowship.

Jesus calls us all unto a table of life where there is enough for everyone, where jugs of water are turned into wine as humanity is married to God. On his knees, before an adulteress he writes, not on stone, but in sand where the wind of time blows away all condemnation and an invitation to newness of life is opened. The guilty male counterpart to the adulteress is missing from the story because in Christ all humanity is become a bride (and because of male duplicity, dominance, and arrogance). God is not in the elements, God is not in the ceremony, God is in the people who give and receive the gift and grace of life freely so that there shall be no poor among us. It is because some have not discerned the needs of others in the body of Christ that there are those among us who are weak, sick and have suffered death.

The Ceremony in Corinthians

It is easily apparent that Paul introduced the communion ceremony in the Corinthian letter in order to get the rich to eat with the poor. The poor suffered illness and early death because of a lack of care. The rich participated in their love feasts unworthily because of their purposeful separation from the poor. Poor people will not share their needs with the rich for many reasons including shame. It is the responsibility of the rich to develop relationships of love with the poor.

I do not think Paul ever intended to remove the ceremony from the love feast. The empty table of the Lord is only a piece of furniture. The sip and the crumb are to be accompanied with a full meal, with conversation about Jesus and his vision for humanity. In this 'Spirit' sharing of the earth's resources abound and the table is filled with food, clothing, debt release, job offers, help for the disabled, educational opportunities etc.

Paul's priority for the Corinthian church was to end social stratification built around wealth and power. During the ceremony we are to remember that humanity continues to kill the Lord through reducing a life sharing communal practice into a sacrament. God is holy and God looks upon human life as sacred. People are sacred not a ceremony. We do not need collared robed priests! We need to love our neighbor enough to gain their trust, hear their need and meet it.

The gospel of John (written later) reflects a non-sacramental community where service to the needy is the role of anyone who would be like Jesus. In John the ceremony is communicated as a spiritual practice made evident through practical acts of loving provision and non-violence.

Beyond the Veil

Imagining the Unimaginable

Total depravity serves no good end
Hope for humanity is Jesus' way
Swing wide O arc for the sake of grace
We shall overcome this condition
One day, today, a day to come

The healing of creation is a moral matter
a reflection of God in humanity
To align one's self with God
To receive of the nature of the holy one
To be conformed to the image of his son

There is only one kingdom come
all others are a lie
Imagine a world without money
It is the unimaginable surety of Jesus' reign

Imagine a world where the sacred is every human being
A world without prisons
Where character formation is grander than science
A world without excess
Imagine a world with no sins to inherit
A world void of violence

Jesus answered, "My kingdom is not from this world. If my kingdom were from this world, my followers would be fighting to keep me from being handed over to the Jews. But as it is, my kingdom is not from here." Pilate asked him, "So you are a king?" Jesus answered, "You say that I am a king. For this I was born, and for this I came into the world, to testify to the truth. Everyone who belongs to the truth listens to my voice."

John 8:36-37

Imagine a World of Peace

To imagine the unimaginable is to be unrealistic in relation to the present accepted norms that constitute how humanity lives under systems and institutions. To imagine the unimaginable is to join God in a hope expressed in visions and dreams and embraced unto death by exemplary people of faith who died rather than succumb to the status quo.

Our initial problem is the excessive consumption of a few who stand over the rest of us and unite us under ideologies of war as an inevitable role of governing and absolutely essential for survival. These Darwinian thinkers promote technological progress as the moral compass that justifies the sacrifice of others, even our own children through warring. In their thought a few must control the earth's resources so that we might advance as a species beyond the need for labor that wears and exhausts the body. Of course along the way they acquire personal wealth and sit as kings over the rest of us.

According to scripture the unifying effort of tower (skyscraper) building and shipping all human resources toward the city is doomed to fail. As long as we differentiate one human being from another by assigning arbitrary value based upon birth right, wealth, or any other divisive factor we will 'speak in differing tongues' due to our separation. This language barrier can never be conquered, language is living and separation causes changes in speech, in value, in meaning.

Humanity is not built in conjunction with technological achievement, humanity progresses only through faith in God that makes the life of every human being sacred and focuses on educating and preparing every human being for living in a moral society where sharing is the norm.

It all begins when we cease to teach our children to war. War is not inevitable once we leave the philosophy of Plato behind and teach our children to live and die for peace without war. It is better to be a martyr for peace than to die for Ceasar's Pax Romana. Peace begins with resistance to all those that choose war, and war is always profitable for the kings of the earth.

A World without Kings

Unfit for Ruling

A World without Kings
Begins with the education of Children
It is the teaching of Torah
The vision of Jesus

The political shaping of reality is idolatrous
Christianity is not a political system
To be aligned with God's reign
Is to be misaligned with the world of Kings

National indoctrination is a crime against the generations
The tool of despots and thieves
The medium of militarism's sorcery
Culminating in child sacrifice

A World of Peace
Begins with the education of children
It is the teaching of Torah
The vision of Jesus

Peace can be taught
Never fought for
After learning history
We only repeat it

The giants of old, mythical souls
Reduced women to objects of desire
Reduced humanity to masses for exploitation
Subjected the earth to the darkness of political violence

Lotteries for souls
Demographic studies
Useless theology
Salvation for the masses
A world without change

Peace can be taught
Never fought for
After learning history
We only repeat it

If only we would teach our children
Oh that we would liberate them from the giants
There is a way
A way of sacredness where human beings
are worth more than giants

But the thing displeased Samuel when they said, "Give us a king to govern us." Samuel prayed to the LORD, and the LORD said to Samuel, "Listen to the voice of the people in all that they say to you; for they have not rejected you, but they have rejected me from being king over them. Just as they have done to me, from the day I brought them up out of Egypt to this day, forsaking me and serving other gods, so also they are doing to you. Now then, listen to their voice; only—you shall solemnly warn them, and show them the ways of the king who shall reign over them."

First Sam 8:7-9

The Servant King

It is not Plato's philosopher king that constitutes Christian ideo-logical views on leadership; rather it is Jesus the servant king. We are our best when we recognize every human being as an object of eternal love (sacred). Once this knowledge enters the soul all self-identity built on pride, arrogance, or through power and wealth is forced to surrender. The author of our faith, the living exemplar, Jesus, defines kingship as an obsolete concept replaced by love and giving to others. The true king is one who models back to people the image of God in humanity. It is God's design that we all mature into servant kings and demonstrate through our lives the (being) Spirit of God in us by overcoming all that halts or hinders human-ity from living together in peace.

The voice of humanity speaks but fails to listen. God speaks and longs to be heard for his way is the way of life.

Trauma the Evil of Human Experience

The Trauma of Jesus

The emotional grips of trauma
dripped from his body like sweat

He cried out father forgive
in his suffering he could not
the dissolution of his self
is his alignment with all victims

His trauma is to never be forgotten
Drink of his blood O guilty one
Until the day of return he will not let us forget

The one who would not pick up a stone
Died betrayed and alone
Excluded from all
An object of horror
God unknown

Before God he lives justified
Before humanity he lives seated in an unseen place

The 'son of man'
the human being
The one emptied of all that it meant to be God
Endured the trauma of evil
Helpless, alone, an innocent victim
Jesus is not a foreigner to suffering trauma
Humanity do you love me?

At three o'clock Jesus cried out with a loud voice, "Eloi, Eloi, lema sabachthani?" which means, "My God, my God, why have you forsaken me?"

Mark 15:34

Trauma, Jesus, and Spirituality

Trauma is a life altering intrusion into the life of a human being. Trauma can cause a complete dissolution of self, leaving a person without a sense of meaning, making their life an unspeakable experience of pain. It appears that Jesus began his ministerial journey with great hope for the emergence of the reign of God that would initiate a new beginning, a power that would transform human reality. However as the gospel stories unfold it becomes apparent that Jesus' hope is altered by the resistance he experiences at every turn.

Although Jesus' displays acts of power that affirm his identity as the son of God, the messiah, neither his family nor his disciples can capture the vision resting in his soul. John the Baptist stumbles at Jesus' approach and cannot conceive how the appearance of the messiah is compatible with the suffering of his own imprisonment and ensuing death. Even in his greatness, there lay in John a zealotry inconsistent with Jesus' vision for the entrance of the reign of God.

Jesus' mother accompanies his siblings and fear that Jesus' commitment to goodness without some form of violent upheaval will lead only to his death and perhaps the persecution of his family and followers. Jesus' approach to reality, his love, his refusal to use his power except to heal the sick all fail to contend with the powers of empire in a direct assault.

Although Mary and John are at Jesus' crucifixion they do not speak. Peter for all his bluster is an unreliable friend to Jesus and his betrayal as predictable as the morning crowing of the rooster. Jesus' self-identity is incompatible with all his relationships; Jesus' stands alone.

Alone in the garden (his disciples are sleeping) Jesus' continues to express a hope for transformation that does not require the trauma of all this betrayal and forthcoming torturous death. The faith of Jesus in God's power to help and in God's will to work in a manner that for Jesus' is becoming incomprehensible and traumatic is expressive as hope's eternal reality; a reality based in God's power and goodness.

Jesus' offered hope to the guilty humanity on a cross alongside him who expressed hope in Jesus' unseen vision of God's reign. Jesus prayed for the father to forgive his torturers because in his moment of suffering he could not. Jesus was rational enough to affirm that they did not know what they were doing (we still do not know).

When trauma is experienced, healing of the victim is not God's gift, rather healing comes from the admission of guilt by the person(s) who caused the trauma. Trauma marks the soul and so Jesus' scars remain visible after the resurrection; awaiting a day when the eyes of those who did not know what they were doing are opened to their sin, their crime.

Even after his resurrection when Jesus' message and way of life is vindicated by God, Jesus' seeks to hear his betraying friend Peter say "Forgive me, I love you, I'm so sorry". Poor Peter can only affirm Jesus' greatness; he cannot hear Jesus' need for his friend to accomplish healing reconciliation with an embrace, tears and words of repentance and love. However, Jesus opens a path for Peter to affirm his love in time by charging Peter to feed (teach) those who like Jesus are non-violent souls; unlike Peter who will need a lifetime before he finally fully embraces Jesus' way. Peter was a slow learner, his propensity for violence is seen in the garden, displayed in words of betrayal and exposed by the first martyr (Stephen) who doesn't seek greatness but waits on widows.

In order for Jesus to be the sole priest before God for all humanity, Jesus needed to face the experience of trauma in all its force and do so in the weakness of flesh with the strength of hope for a better day beyond the grave. In Christ Jesus, God has experienced human trauma and knows the pain, the dissolution, the need for the perpetrator(s) to reconcile.

The scars of trauma are not easily healed. They remain as constant reminders of heinous acts of inhumane treatment. The effects of trauma can re-visit a human being after years of living when it is thought they have conquered the once beleaguering power that harmed their soul. Trauma intrudes upon God's work of grace in a life because one day the guilty will face their victims and hear their stories and if they are to enter the kingdom of God they must ask for forgiveness.

Speaking God's Word

At the Limits of Understanding

At the limits of understanding
Where revelation overwhelms
Where innumerable thoughts pass through the soul
I lift my hands
My heart beats
I am changed
I cannot recall all that I thought

This divine touch seeds the soul
Hidden within like treasure for another day
The body of flesh holds a gift
A gift waiting to speak
Needing only the moment

Words of truth deposited within
God's Spirit shakes them loose
The lips quiver with power
God's words
Will they dare to question again?

The indomitable wisdom of the living Christ
Alive in his own
Will they respond with repentance or stones?
Truth spoken that demands change or rejection
Violence or transformation

God has entered the world
Words spoken in flesh

When they hand you over, do not worry about how you are to
speak or what you are to say; for what you are to say will be given
to you at that time;

Matt 10:19

That all God's People would become Prophets

We should not think that speaking for God is merely a miraculous
event that occurs without preparation. Rather, we must under-
stand that God works with our person with who we are, we give
what is within us. As God's children we fill ourselves with truth
and understanding. We do not need to memorize stock responses
to questions in order to defend ourselves against charges before
persecutors. If we have meditated upon the word, wrestled with re-
ality, thought theologically, and sought to love in the face of all the
surrounding wickedness, then we will find ourselves illuminated
and free of tongue to speak truth spontaneously.

It is said of the prophets that the messenger and the message
were one. Truly this statement affirms an inner formation of heart,
mind and character that is ready to be 'spirited' by the Lord to
speak. Moses' desired that all God's people be so formed in their
inner self that they could speak for God. Conformation to the im-
age of God's son is the work of the Holy Spirit and the result is a
person ready to engage the powers with truth.

Living Truth

Freedom and Truth

Truth is a disruptive power in the world
Liberation from perceived normalcy
Freedom from
Freedom to
A dizzying experience

Like a crushed vessel
Am I being molded or destroyed
Yet the mind and spirit grow like an Oak
Perhaps I'll just dance with the wind
and think till dawn

Captured in the complexity of simplicity
Shall I cry or laugh?
Perhaps I'll just sing a song
and meditate all night long

A single sentence possessing immeasurable truth
A single life living free embodying truth
He was more than normalcy could endure
Can I endure his baptism?
This immersion in truth pulls me forward

Truth is the sweetness between life and death
Where flesh becomes spirit
The freedom to live
The freedom to die

Roaring like a lion
Captured by a lamb
Truth completes man and woman

My vision has increased
I can see him
but not yet
The shattering events of life
with death and sorrow
turn now and lift me up

The trauma of rising above a world below
The arms of truth open paradise for his children
Where is God when suffering cries out?
Where tombs are turned into gardens
Where death is the bridge to life
Learning to know the truth is impossible without pain

Shall I cry out?
Surely the religious would be offended at my boldness
The honesty of brokenness is music in the ears of God
Let the earth quake and the day turn to night
Truth rolls through death's door

and you will know the truth, and the truth will make you free.
John 8:32

The Trauma of Truth

Failure is a part of life; it is inescapable. We learn best through sur-
viving failure and other calamities that produce pain and suffering.
Out of enduring faith the indomitable power of hope transforms
us into spiritual people. Isaiah 49:1-4 expresses the feelings of Jesus
in relation to the work of his life. This is understood because Jesus'
fulfills the calling of Israel and so embodies the ideal of Israel's
calling as a people.

Isaiah 49:1

Listen to me, O coastlands,
pay attention, you peoples from far away!
The LORD called me before I was born,
while I was in my mother's womb he named me.

He made my mouth like a sharp sword,
in the shadow of his hand he hid me;
he made me a polished arrow,
in his quiver he hid me away.

And he said to me, "You are my servant,
Israel, in whom I will be glorified."

But I said, "I have labored in vain,
I have spent my strength for nothing and vanity;
yet surely my cause is with the LORD,
and my reward with my God."

Certainly at the end of his life, Jesus' experience with his dis-
ciples was filled with disappointment. Living in a world of human
beings it is inevitable that we who try to communicate Jesus' vi-
sion of reality will experience both personal failure and the failure
of those we know. We cannot measure our life in successes, rather
the measure of life is revealed in how we overcome the failure
of both others and ourselves. Or as it is written 'Love covers a
multitude of sins'.

It is apparent that loving human beings requires some form
of personal death on the part of the lover. It is easier to give love

in such a way when we recognize our own limitations, our own failures. Sin is always a position before God, but in relation to one another our lives intertwine in unintended but conflicting ways where hurt is inevitable. It is the lack of God in the world that results in this condition; only 'in Christ' can we overcome the human condition and function in liberating love.

Made in the USA
Lexington, KY
21 November 2018